Twayne's English Authors Series

EDITOR OF THIS VOLUME

Herbert Sussman

Northeastern University

Katharine Tynan

TEAS 272

Katharine Tynan

KATHARINE TYNAN

By ANN CONNERTON FALLON

TWAYNE PUBLISHERS
A DIVISON OF G. K. HALL & CO., BOSTON

Published in 1979 by Twayne Publishers,
A Division of G. K. Hall & Co.
All Rights Reserved

Printed on permanent/durable acid-free paper and bound
in the United States of America

First Printing

Library of Congress Cataloging in Publication Data

Fallon, Ann Connerton.
Katharine Tynan.

(Twayne's English authors series ; TEAS 272)
Bibliography: p. 182 - 87
Includes index.
1. Hinkson, Katharine Tynan, 1861 - 1931—Criticism
and interpretation.
PR4790.H3Z67   821'.9'12   79-12331
ISBN 0-8057-6754-1

To My Parents

Contents

About the Author

Ann Connerton Fallon studied English and Classics at Boston University. As an undergraduate she attended Trinity College Dublin as a special student for one year. In 1971 she received her B.A. summa cum laude from Boston University and was elected to Phi Beta Kappa. In the following year she returned to Trinity College where she prepared her thesis on the classical influences in Keats's poetry and was awarded the degree of M. Litt.

She continued her studies in literature at Brandeis University, Waltham, Mass., where she received the M.A., and is currently completing her dissertation for the Ph.D.

As a graduate student she taught freshman seminars at Brandeis University and has also taught at Newbury Junior College, Boston, and at the Dublin Institute of Adult Education. She has written many reviews in her fields of academic interest: Anglo-Irish literature and literary biography. Ann Connerton Fallon is currently living in Dublin, Ireland, and is researching a study of W. B. Yeats's early prose fiction.

Preface

Katharine Tynan is remembered today as a leading member of the Irish literary movement which developed in the last decade of the nineteenth century. In this context she is also remembered as a close friend and literary associate of William Butler Yeats. She was also a good minor poet in her own right, and her work, both within the Irish literary movement and outside it, deserves more critical attention than it has yet received.

Throughout her long career Katharine Tynan published over two hundred titles, including volumes of poetry, novels, plays, autobiographical works, and commemorations. She also edited and wrote the introductions to a number of other works. These two hundred titles do not include the hundreds of sketches, reviews, interviews, and columns she contributed to countless contemporary popular journals and magazines.

In keeping with this enormous corpus is the fact that she was one of the few women of her time and generation to support herself by her own writing. And more than this, her writing career gave her entry not only into the male-dominated profession of writing, but into that very life-style once considered the private and enviable domain of the writer. She had access to the social life of the writer—the literary circles, the publishers' parties, the traveling abroad, the social acceptance into all ranks of society, the fame and the notoriety of the established and successful writer. For the daughter of the gentleman farmer from the Irish countryside, a girl with little formal education, nearly blind, and of plain appearance, this success was achieved by a very remarkable personality.

For the reader unfamiliar with Tynan's life and works, it is necessary to remember that, like the "remarkable Jane" Austen whom she admired—Tynan wrote of what she knew. Her poem "Apologia," the prefatory poem to her *Ballads and Lyrics* (1891), which was much admired by her good friend, W. B. Yeats, tells the reader of her poetry what to expect and not to expect:

Here in my book there will be found
No gleanings from a foreign ground:
The quiet thoughts of one whose feet
Have scarcely left her green retreat.

So in my book there will be found
No gleanings from a foreign ground.
If such you seek, go buy, go buy
Of some more travelled folk than I.

Kind Master Critic, say not, please,
How that her world so narrow is,
Since here she warns expectant eyes
But homely is her merchandise.

Her life and work are inextricably woven together and, consequently, I have tried to indicate in the following chapters the close relationship between the events of her life and the novels and poetry she wrote using those life experiences. The enormous number of books which Tynan produced poses a problem to the modern reader and critic. I have dealt fairly fully with those books on which her early reputation rests—her first three volumes of poetry which link her to the Irish literary movement. Thereafter, I have studied the individual volumes of poetry, referring wherever possible to those poems which have since been published in the two modern collections edited by George Russell and by Monk Gibbon and which may be more accessible to the reader. Of the many novels I have chosen a representative number which should indicate Tynan's intentions and style in writing fiction. The remaining chapters deal with her works of nonfiction.

My primary intention in this study is to examine Tynan's identity as an Irish writer. This was early established by her first publications and her association with Yeats. In addition, I hope to present to the modern reader the life and significant works of a good minor poet, recognized in her time but neglected in recent years. Her life as a woman of letters, and the work she produced to support and maintain both her reputation and her life-style are of intrinsic interest and of value in understanding the role and position of the woman writer in the literary world.

ANN CONNERTON FALLON

Acknowledgments

I wish to thank Pamela Hinkson for her permission to quote from the published works of her mother, Katharine Tynan Hinkson; Senator Michael Yeats for his permission to quote from the *Letters to Katharine Tynan*, ed. Roger McHugh (Dublin: Clonmore and Reynolds, Ltd., 1953); and Mrs. Norah Tynan Wayte for permission to use a portrait of Katharine Tynan in her possession as the frontispiece of this book.

Chronology

1861   January 23, Katharine born in Dublin to Andrew and Elizabeth Tynan, fourth daughter and one of eleven children.

1868   Tynan family moves to Whitehall, Clondalkin, County Dublin.

1871   August, leaves Whitehall to attend boarding school at the Siena Convent, Drogheda.

1874   August, finishes schooling at the Siena Convent and returns to Whitehall as her father's companion.

1878   Begins to write poetry for her own enjoyment.

1885   June, *Louise de la Valliere*, first book of poetry.

1885   Meets William Butler Yeats through a mutual acquaintance when she is twenty-four and Yeats is twenty.

1887   *Shamrocks*, second book of poetry.

1888   *Poems and Ballads of Young Ireland*, the first joint effort of the Irish literary revival.

1891   *Ballads and Lyrics* and *A Nun, Her Friends and Her Order*, her first book of prose.

1893   May, marries Henry Albert Hinkson in London and begins her residence in England where her five children are born, three of whom survive.

1894   *A Cluster of Nuts*, first collection of short fiction.

1896   *A Lover's Breast-Knot*, a collection of love poems.
        Oh, What a Plague Is Love, the third of the more than hundred novels she was to publish.

1912   Henry Hinkson appointed resident magistrate in Ireland. The family prepares to move from England to Ireland.

1913   *Twenty-Five Years*, the first of her five volumes of reminiscences.

1914   Travels to Rome with friends to observe the International Women's Congress. The Hinkson family is settled in Castlebar, County Mayo, where Henry takes up his duties.

1916   Easter Rising takes place in Dublin. *The Middle Years,* the second volume of her memoirs.

1919   Henry Hinkson dies in County Mayo. Tynan begins her years of travel. *The Years of the Shadow,* third volume of her memoirs.

1922   Tynan visits Cologne, Germany, during the Occupation. *The Wandering Years.*

1924   *Memories,* an additional volume of reminiscences.

1925   *Life in the Occupied Area,* based on her German experiences.

1927   *Twilight Songs,* the last of her many volumes of poetry. Continues her visits to England and Ireland, and her novel writing.

1931   April 2, Katharine Tynan dies in London and is buried there.

CHAPTER 1

A Green Retreat

KATHARINE Tynan's story begins with her father. Andrew Tynan not only figured in her life as parent and provider of a comfortable home, but also shaped her tastes, set her standards of behavior, launched her upon a literary career, and left a marked influence on her personal life which governed that which she wrote and thought.

Tynan devotes long sections of her autobiographical writings to her father; he appears as a character in some of her sketches and novels; he even appears, as she notes herself, in W. B. Yeats's early short story, "A Knight of the Sheep." Some of her most affecting poetry is addressed to him or speaks of him. Much of this chapter deals with Tynan's relationship with her father, because it was to remain the central relationship of her long life. For a true understanding of her later relationships with men and women, and for an insight into her work and thought, it is necessary to examine the influences which shaped her life.

Of Andrew Tynan's background we have the statements of his daughter in her autobiographical works, *Twenty Five Years* and *Memories* in particular. Andrew Tynan's mother, a Catholic and an only child, eloped in the early nineteenth century and married a young Dublin Protestant (called Tynan)in a Protestant church. Mixed marriages between Catholic and Protestant were rare in Ireland, and strongly disapproved of, in this case, by the girl's parents. However, when young Mr. Tynan died, leaving a widow and two children, Mrs. Tynan returned to her parents' home where the children were accepted and raised by the grandparents under their name. Andrew Tynan was still a child when his mother died and he grew up on his grandparents' farm in Cheeverstown, County Dublin. On reaching maturity, he assumed the name of Tynan once again and moved to Dublin.

Tynan always writes of her father with deep affection and an appreciation of his generous, ebullient, kind, and amiable personality. Of the numerous people of whom she writes in her memoirs and reminiscences, her father is the most carefully drawn and well developed character of them all.

Of her father's country origins, she writes in *Memories:*

He was a countryman bred and born, though he came to the city from the mountains of Wicklow, and remained there for many years before he became a countryman again. Although he was a countryman he had a natural zest for the life and eventfulness of the old city of Dublin—for the politics, the amusements, the social life of the city. Over the fire at night he would recreate it all for me, or when I drove with him over the fields he loved as though they were flesh and blood, behind his little pony. He made a good many of my opinions during the years when I was pretty constantly his companion.[1]

I   *Katharine Tynan's Background*

Andrew Tynan married Elizabeth Reily and they raised eleven children, of whom Katharine Tynan was the fourth daughter, born on January 23, 1861. Tynan's attitude toward her mother, as displayed in the autobiographical writings, is intriguing. She tells us little about her mother, but what she does reveal points to the basis of that intense relationship Tynan developed with her father: "My mother was a simple, innocent, narrow woman, with whose milk-maid large beauty he had fallen in love with as a young man, but I think they hardly ever met on the same plane of thought. She counts for no more in my life that was full of him, than if she had been a person in a book."[2]

Compared to her numerous and detailed descriptions of her father, those which deal with her mother are both scanty and vague. Although written when she herself was in middle age, they recall the sense of disappointment and consequent hostility the adolescent Tynan directed at her mother. She writes that ". . . mother was a large, placid woman, who became an invalid at an early age and influenced my life hardly at all. While I was still very little, before the family had grown, before there was an invalid mother, I have beautiful memories of my father."[3]

In these passages about Tynan's early life, her mother always suffers by comparison with her father. Elizabeth Tynan was neither jovial nor sociable; she did not drive out to the mountains in the little pony cart or picnic with her children. "She would probably stay at home to look after her brood. She was the mid-Victorian woman, and found an engrossing occupation in being the mother of eleven."[4]

In these and other passages Tynan tends to identify strongly with her father, the sociable, strong, friendly, nature loving man, and detach herself from the mother whom she characterizes as a woman isolated, and limited by a life completely devoted to bearing and raising children. This detachment is so strong that she hardly mentions her mother's death and its effects, although she refers often to her father's death and her great personal loss. Similarly, she seldom mentions her brothers and sisters and, consequently, the reader of Tynan's memoirs is not presented with a rounded picture of her childhood in relation to her family other than her father. This conscious neglect is significant in a writer who wrote so frankly about herself and her friends and acquaintances. Her feelings and emotions in regard to her father, to Yeats, and even to dead heroes such as the Irish patriot, Lord Edward Fitzgerald, are presented with an immediacy that is totally absent from her mention of her mother or her siblings.

In addition to this relationship with her parents, other significant events stand out in Tynan's early emotional and physical life. One of these was Andrew Tynan's decision to move his family from the city of Dublin to Clondalkin, County Dublin. The house, called Whitehall, was to be Katharine Tynan's home from early childhood until her marriage in 1893, and still stands today in the midst of a developing suburb of Dublin.

But in 1868 the lands around the house were still agricultural, rolling fields running away to the hills. Katharine Tynan loved Whitehall with a passion, "the small cottage building with little windows under immense over-hanging eaves of thatch and a hall door within a porch of green trellis."[5]

She had by her own account a happy childhood and youth in that house, and she writes of that period—of a child's exploration of nature in the lands surrounding the charming house—frequently and with obvious delight and nostalgia:

Of Whitehall as it was then I could write many pages without hoping to capture the glamour, for that was in the child's mind. It had everything

to delight a child. . . . Whitehall, as we came to it, was a truly
delightful abode. I have said it had all the amenities for children: nor
was it lonely, for on the other side of the red-tiled kitchen, with the two
little windows and the door opening onto the grass and divided only by
a partition wall, dwelt Dan Kinsella with his wife and children.[6]

The years at Whitehall are marked in Tynan's memory by her
father's varying success as farmer and business man. Initially, he
had moderate success in his ventures but as time passed,
adversity set in. During those early years she did not know her
father well because they had not, as she says, "discovered one
another."[7] It was not until Katharine Tynan finished her formal
schooling that father and daughter became the remarkable
companions she portrays in her memoirs.

Her early education had been begun at a Miss M'Cabe's, an
infant school to which she was sent to keep her from underfoot in
the steadily growing household.[8] In the cosy atmosphere of Miss
M'Cabe's she became proficient in spelling and consequently in
reading. This school was in the city of Dublin, and her early
education came to an end with the removal of the family to
Whitehall. A number of years later, in August, 1871, she was sent
as a boarding pupil to the Siena Convent in Drogheda, some sixty
miles from Dublin, at the suggestion of a friend of her father who
saw that she was "running wild." According to the school's
account books, she stayed as a student until August, 1874.[9]

She describes the school as "a green garden-place of quiet
restfulness"[10] where she "only learned what I wanted to and that
was not very much."[11] After a house full of small children, Tynan
found the convent school a place of peace and contentment, and,
as a result, developed in three short years a lifelong respect and
affection for the life of the convent and the nuns who lived there.
This love, and her knowledge of the inner workings of convent
life, especially the order and cleanliness, inform many passages
in her later novels.

Tynan was withdrawn from this school at the age of fourteen,
at which time her formal education came to an abrupt end. She
was removed from the school "wholly and solely, I believe,
because my father wanted my society."[12]

This change in her relationship with her father came about for
two reasons. The first was the death of his older daughter, Mary,
his favorite child whom he loved because of her "soft beauty and

tenderness." Mary was entering adulthood as her mother declined into an invalidism leading to her eventual early death. Mary stood out from the rabble of the younger children, quiet, innocent, pursuing her painting and needlework and preparing herself to enter a convent as a nun. She died suddenly and unexpectedly in the summer preceding her entry into the novitiate. It was Katharine's first personal experience of loss and death, and the sudden loss of her beloved and admired older sister affected her deeply. Unfortunately, it was to be the first of the many serious losses of loved ones in Tynan's life. Of her sister she writes:

She was just a brief lovely vision. . . . She knew that I adored her and she petted me. She let me see just a glimpse of her supernatural secret. It made me determined to be a nun, and the determination lasted for a good dozen years afterwards. There was something heavenly in the vision, something of long convent corridors, dazzlingly clean, flooded with light and air, sweet with the smell of lilies and a thought of incense, of little convent cells naked and pure, of convent gardens, places where "The Brides of Christ/Lie hid, emparadised."[13]

Although Tynan does not refer to her sister Mary again, except to say that she eventually replaced Mary in her father's affections, the character of Mary can be discerned in any number of the novels where one of the female characters is called by her vocation to the convent. Nor did Tynan, although she did not enter a convent, ever lose her early affection and feeling for the life behind walls, and the convent is often figured in her novels as a place of peace, solitude, and sometimes joy for those characters wishing to escape from the world, or to repent, or to wed themselves in solitary bliss to a higher ideal. Her highest compliment to nuns, both in her fiction and nonfiction, is the repeated comment that they retained their childlike qualities of innocent and simple pleasure and an ignorance of the ways of the world. Indeed, she often attributes these same qualities to the priests of her acquaintance and of her novels. They too pleased her with their boyishness, as she terms it, and their boyish love of jokes and sense of humor.[14]

Following Mary's death came a decline in the financial situation of the family. Mrs. Tynan died young, and while the younger children were sent away to school the older children went out into the world. During this period, Katharine Tynan, one sister, and a maidservant, lived at Whitehall while Andrew Tynan traveled on business connected with his farming. In this lonely time she read unceasingly any books she found available to her in her isolation.

Andrew Tynan had spent his fortune on scientific farming methods. He loved his lands and made them rich and fruitful. He held the contracts to supply live cattle from his lands to the British army in England and in Ireland. However, as she writes, "He did it alone and it was too much for him," and he lost a small fortune over the army contracts.[15]

However, he did not lose all of his money, and enough was left for him to return to Whitehall where he lived until his death. The lands were sold after his death and used as an aerodrome in World War I and, later, as a camp for the new army of the Irish Republic. The house was maintained by one of Katharine's sisters after Mr. Tynan's death.

Fat and lean years had alternated until the financial matters settled. Although not rich, the Tynans were of the gentleman farmer class. As a well-traveled and well-read man with sophisticated taste, Mr. Tynan introduced his daughter to a world beyond Whitehall. However, before this happy time she suffered another major occurrence in her young life.

In 1867, just before the move to Whitehall, Tynan began gradually to become blind, and suffered near total blindness until 1869. Her condition was despaired of by the family and by the doctors. However, her father refused to give up hope and he brought her to numerous doctors, finally finding one to help them in Harcourt Street in Dublin. Katharine Tynan writes with feeling: "I keep his name in grateful memory. I remember the double hall doors of his home that opened to receive us. I remember . . . the consulting room, where the doctor's finger and thumb lifted the eyelids that it was torture to keep open. Nothing more than that; but presently I was reading again and the darkness was a family tradition."[16]

The darkness, as she calls it, was apparently caused by ulcers on the eyes. Although her sight returned, it was never fully restored. She wore glasses all of her life and describes herself frequently as being purblind. She was dim-sighted and short-sighted, and, as a result, came to depend on those around her, particularly her friends, for assistance in any form of traveling.

Her eyesight worsened in later life and she was often unable to recognize the faces of old friends. She remained convinced, however, that her bad eyesight had brought her many friends and experiences she might otherwise have missed, because it had often rendered her helpless and dependent on those around her, and she believed this brought her closer to them. Her attitude of courage and optimism in regard to her eyesight is characteristic of the way in which Tynan approached the many challenges which her life presented her.

Before Tynan had reached the age of eighteen she had experienced a childhood and youth of intense, sometimes extreme events. She was a child whose birthdate was lost because there were eleven to remember;[17] a child sent away to a pleasant school to be kept out of the way; a child exposed to the realities of life at an early age:

There are highlights in the mists and shadows and all else in between is lost. I was brought up on the dreadful churchyard stories of the Irish peasant imagination. We used to creep up the dark stairs to bed in a shivering string, each child trying to be in the middle and not at either end. Of course, I was taken to a wake. I saw more dead people in my youth than I ever did as an adult. The nurse took us to a wake . . . I can recall even now the yellow sharpened face of the dead man. There was a plate of salt on his breast, pennies on his eyelids to keep them closed, pipes, tobacco, and snuff on a table at the bed's foot.[18]

Impressions like these were never lost. Throughout her life, Tynan was afraid of the dark, particularly as she fell to sleep. She suffered from blindness at a formative age. Her mother, whom Tynan had perceived as distant and aloof, died at an early age. She lost her beloved older sister. It was only then that her personality began to emerge from those of the family around her. And it emerged in the strong light of her father's fondness for her, his liking for her companionship, and his encouragement of her social, cultural, and intellectual life. Through the vicissitudes of her early life, her father stood out as the one constant factor, and the one person responsible for making that life a happy one.

As she grew older, Tynan also became the companion of her father's social life. Andrew Tynan loved society and he was fond of women, their personalities, their feminine ways, their conversation. A new and happy period in Tynan's life had begun:

Then began the good years. . . . These early and middle Summers of
the Seventies weather, when, to use my father's phrase, the sun was
splitting the trees, were golden; but I remember best the Winters. I
think my father's affairs were in such a way that he had a mind at ease.
Like a great many Irishmen he had a passion for the theatre which had
been starved since he had lived in the country. He could never bear to
go anywhere alone; in my society he recaptured the old joys.[19]

Tynan describes their trips to Dublin, where they stayed in the
best hotels, wined and dined, enjoying the theater and all which
the capital city had to offer. He bought her beautiful and
expensive clothing, and introduced her to a social life that
harmonized with the ease of living at Whitehall during the good
days.

II *Tynan's Education and Formative Reading*

When Katharine Tynan was in her teens, Andrew Tynan
undertook the completion of her education:

It was my father who brought books into the house, miscellaneous lots
picked up at auctions, of the most varied kind. He had no belief in
censorship. I cannot recall that he ever told me not to read any book,
although I must have read some curious ones under his eyes. If he gave
my reading direction it was towards poetry—Irish National poetry for
the most part and often turgid stuff, although of an unimpeachable
loftiness of tone.[20]

She writes that as a child she had been a voracious reader
despite her poor eyesight. It was thought at the time that she had
ruined her eyes by too much reading and had been forbidden for
some period in her early childhood to read. But as her eyesight
recovered, she returned to a habit which she maintained
throughout her life.

She read with little method or guidance the books that were
made available to her through her father, his friends, or the
libraries of the period. Mrs. Atkinson and Count Plunkett, friends
of the family, gave her an assortment of books, among them
Patmore's *Odes* and Keats' poetry. She lists other books, an odd
mixture of fiction and nonfiction, including *Nicholas Nickleby*,
Fanny Burney's *Cecilia*, *The Arabian Nights*, and *Uncle Tom's
Cabin*. She read some Maria Edgeworth, although not the

outstanding *Castle Rackrent.*[21] Books such as these, she says, gave her mind a distinct bent toward the eighteenth century.[22]

Even then, in those early years, she noticed that quality of novels which made them escapes for the imagination. They were also items to be treasured in themselves and she recalls years later the texture, the colors, the paper of which they were made. In her father's house she had available to her both the current Irish and English periodicals, and these, too, opened up new worlds to her imagination.

Under her father's guidance she read, and developed a deep love for, poetry of all kinds:

I read all the modern poetry I could get my hands on. I read Swinburne from beginning to end, and was at once alarmed and fascinated by him. . . . I was starved for poetry. The fascination of Swinburne, Morris, Rossetti, was yet about us. Poetry was being read by anybody who had pretensions to good taste. The young men at Oxford and Cambridge were reading poetry, as were their sisters in parsonages and the houses of the professional classes.[23]

III *Beginning of Her Poetic Career*

During this period of her late teens, during which she enjoyed the pleasures and security of a sheltered and secure life, reading, going about with her father to the theater, meeting his friends and enjoying his society, she turned her thoughts to attempting some poetry of her own: "Somewhere about 1878 I wrote my first poem. Doubtless I should have made many essays before that date . . . if I had been brought up in a literary atmosphere. That I was not was doubtless to my benefit, for my critical faculty had more time to grow. I had plenty of poor and weak influences to shed. If I had written earlier I should perhaps not have begun to discover that they were poor and weak."[24] She continued to write poetry from this time and in the early 1880s began to write for publication. It was the beginning of a lifelong career, unbroken by illness, marriage, children, or her travels.

I will now hark back to the beginnings of my own literary career. . . . My first important literary event was the beginning of my friendship with Father Matthew Russell S. J. . . . I had already gathered a few sheaves—a few poems in the *Graphic*, the Sonnet in the *Spectator*, verses here and there in Dublin newspapers, when I had the happy thought, for me, of sending a poem to the *Irish Monthly*.[25]

Through her publication in the *Irish Monthly* and her friendship
with Father Russell, its editor, she was launched on a literary
career in Dublin. Her name became known, and she met and
became friends with many young people in the political, social,
and literary arena of Dublin. From this fortunate meeting with
Father Russell her circle widened and with it, her own
experience of life. Early publication and fame are exciting to any
young writer, but to a sheltered young Irish Catholic girl it was a
liberating experience. Suddenly, social standards that applied to
her contemporaries no longer applied to her: "From about 1884 I
had really begun to live. I had found out what I could do, and
being regarded as an exceptional person at home and abroad, I
had perfect freedom about my actions. I had as many masculine
friends as I liked, and saw as much of them as I wished."[26] She
elaborates further:

I had found myself. Friendships were springing up on every side. My
father was inordinately pleased with me, and did everything he could
to make my life run smoothly for me. I had emerged from the class to
whom poetry meant little or nothing—the middle class is the same
everywhere—and I had formed a little circle of my own. There were
always two sets of guests in those days at the Sunday parties which were
a feature in my old home. There were friends and there were my
sister's friends. My friends used to gather in the little room my father's
love had made beautiful. We used to talk literature endlessly.[27]

This long and happy period of Tynan's life began in earnest with
the publication of her first book of poetry, her first book, in fact,
of more than two hundred.

    Louise de la Valliere appeared in June, 1885. It was a
collection of poems, many of which had appeared in newspapers
and magazines, and for the publication of which her father paid
twenty pounds sterling—a large sum in those days. It was a
commercial success at once, being bought out by her circle of
literary friends.[28] The critical and financial success of the book
which, she notes herself, was probably not worthy of it, brought
herself and her father great happiness and satisfaction. With the
publication of the book her fame in Dublin spread and her home
became on Sundays a literary salon.

    Sundays at Whitehall had always been a social event. Andrew
Tynan's many friends came to call and good food, good fires, and

good conversation were always to be found there. Andrew Tynan's interests were political, and those Sunday discussions did much to inform the young Tynan of the political situation in Ireland at that time as well as in years gone by. As Tynan established her own circle, her young literary friends came and talked of literature with her and of politics with her amiable father. Because of this firmly established social tradition, and because of his unfailing interest in Tynan's life and career, Andrew Tynan converted a room in the house in Clondalkin for her exclusive use. From this time until her marriage and move to England in 1893, this room was the focal point of her social and intellectual life, and in fact for many of the young writers she knew. She writes at length of this room in her autobiographical works, describing it in minute detail, and never failing to note her gratitude to her father who provided this ideal setting for the development of her social life and career. Among the many people who passed through that salon were a number whose success and fame were to outweigh those of Katharine Tynan. Among them were W. B. Yeats, Douglas Hyde, and George Russell, later known as A. E.

In Douglas Hyde's diaries of the period he records his own impressions of those Sunday afternoons at Whitehall. Hyde was then a serious student at Trinity College, Dublin, and a member of that larger social and literary set to which Tynan belonged. Hyde notes at least ten meetings with Katharine Tynan spanning the years 1886 to 1889. On January 23, 1887, he writes:

Yeats the poet called in to me and we walked the four miles to Katherine [sic] Tynan's house at Clondalkin; her four sisters, a brother and her father, an old man, were there. They were at dinner when we arrived and we sat in with them. Katherine showed me her own room, her pictures, books, etc., and I had a long conversation with all of them. They all have a frightful brogue. Her father is a farmer with three hundred acres. . . .[29]

Two days later he writes of her visit to Trinity College in the heart of the city of Dublin, where he was then a student. As a Protestant and member of an old family of the landed gentry, Hyde came from what was then to be considered the upper class of Irish society and his remarks highlight the great divisions between classes in Ireland.

Of this second meeting, Hyde writes:

I met Katherine Tynan and her sister by arrangement at 2:15. I brought them around the college and showed them everything, and all the time I was terribly embarrassed lest anyone should see me talking to them. Katherine was all right but her sister was a sight. I gave them tea, cakes and sweets, etc., and Yeates [sic] came in at the same time.[30]

As a budding nationalist and an aspiring man of letters Hyde frequented the same social circles as Tynan and they met at the homes of mutual acquaintances, especially at John O'Leary's house. Hyde continued to visit her literary salon despite her frightful brogue, and the following entries in his diary give a colorful picture of those Sunday afternoons of which she was so proud:

9 Dec. 1887. Sunday. After Chapel I brought Sheehan with me and we walked to Katherine Tynan's. We arrived there about 3:30 and found Yeats and a friend of his, Russell, an art-student, there before us. There was also two sisters, Misses Lynch, from Dun Laoghaire, one of whom spoke intelligently enough. She had lived in the Aegean and in Greece for a long time, and spoke modern Greek. She had written a novel. Dinner with Katherine and a very long talk with her father. . . .[31]

15 April 1888. Sunday. Chapel in College. Afterwards I walked with Sheehan to Katherine Tynan's. It was a beautiful day. There were a lot of people there. We had dinner and a good talk. We started for home at 10:30 and I took a good stiff drink. Gregg and Johnson from Ballykilbeg and a man named Piper were with us and we walked home singing and shouting as I had never done in my life before. It was a natural reaction to K. T.'s aestheticism![32]

24 February 1889. Katherine Tynan invited me to go out to her so I got up early, went to College chapel and then took a tram to Rathmines where I met a young man from the college named Hinkson and his sister (a B.A. from the 'Royal'). We went together on the steam-tram to Tallaght and from there we walked with a man by the name of Dallinger (an Englishman) to the house of the poetess. A good dinner and much talk, etc., etc.[33]

Douglas Hyde was to go on to achieve great fame. His most influential work was done in the Irish language which he learned from the laborers on his father's estate. He became the founder of the Gaelic League, an organization which worked to restore the use of the Irish language as the national language of the country. He made valuable collections of Irish language stories and poems which he published together with his beautiful translations. He was eventually to become the first president of the new Irish Republic. Although already a published poet, Tynan had much to learn from the work of her acquaintance, Douglas Hyde. W. B. Yeats, who knew them both well, tells us that: "No living Irish poet has learned so much from the translators as Mrs. Hinkson (as she was soon to be known) and the great change this knowledge has made on her verse is an example of the necessity for Irish writers to study native tradition of expression. . . ."[34]

Hyde mentions in his diary entry his meeting with a young Mr. Hinkson. Tynan tells us very little concerning her meeting with her future husband. It can be assumed that, given the freedom of movement her fame had brought her and the wide circle of friends who came to her Sundays at Whitehall, that she met the young, Protestant, Trinity College student through her acquaintances attending that college.

Henry Albert Hinkson was born in March, 1865, to John and Jane Hinkson and he grew up in Rathmines, a suburb of Dublin. He attended The High School, a private secondary school where he took, according to the records, final exams in Greek, Latin, English, and mathematics in the year 1881.[35] He attended the school for five years and left in October, 1882. He entered Trinity College Dublin in 1886 and won a scholarship to study classics in 1888. He formally severed his connection with the college in 1894, apparently without taking a degree.[36] He published a number of books during this period, one an illustrated paperback of the history of Trinity College, written from a student's point of view.[37] Another volume, *Dublin Verses By Members of Trinity College*, which he edited and published in 1895, gives a fair idea, from its list of contributors, of the social circle in which he and Tynan moved during the 1880s. The list includes many of those Trinity students who were to play their own part in the Irish literary revival of which Yeats was to become the notable leader.[38]

Yeats had attended The High School in Dublin but not during the years Henry Hinkson was a student there. In July, 1891, he writes from London to Tynan to inform her that he had asked a mutual friend and former student of the school, Charles

Johnston, if he remembered a boy by the name of Hinkson. Yeats
was pleased to tell her that Johnston had said he did and that he
was a very nice fellow and had the "true instinct of the
scholar."[39] From Yeats' letter one can assume that Tynan had
written to her friend, Yeats, concerning Hinkson and possibly
their forthcoming plans to marry. Of all her literary circle of
young men she was possibly closest to Yeats, and it is significant
that she wrote to him about Hinkson as early as 1891.

IV *Marriage*

Tynan says almost nothing about her courtship and decision to
marry Hinkson. He was Protestant, four years younger than
herself and a scholarly man. She was thirty-two and slightly
plump at the time of her marriage. She wore her hair in a short
fringe across her forehead with the rest tumbling down her back.
Although shy, she gave the impression of being a dominant
personality.[40] A published author who earned her living by her
writing, she was independent and popular with men and women
alike, both as a friend and as a literary personality.

She tells little of those days in her otherwise frank memoirs.
She left Dublin, her family, her pretty room, and her beloved
father behind her. She writes of the day of her departure on the
boat for London, that she stood on deck as long as she could see
her father waving to her from the pier.[41] In May, 1893, she was
married in London from the house of her English friends, Alice
and Wilfred Meynell.[42] The decision to live in England, far from
all that she loved, and far from the burgeoning Irish literary
movement in which she played her part, is never adequately
explained. It can be assumed, however, that both her career and
that of her husband played the major part in their decision.
Tynan would have easy access to her publishers in London and
also to the large reading audience which she was beginning to
develop. In addition, she was available and in contact with the
many magazines and newspapers for which she wrote con-
tinuously at this time in her career.

Her husband had obtained his B.A. degree in classics in 1887
from the Royal University, and he took an M.A. degree in 1890.[43]
He was called to the bar of the Inner Temple in London in
January 1902 and thereafter was known to be a barrister-at-law,
although Tynan does not mention his actively practicing law in

England.[44] He did become a "crammer" or private tutor to boys hoping for a career with the British army, and during their years in England Hinkson also published a number of romantic and historical novels.[45]

One substantial book arose out of Hinkson's experience as a barrister and a novelist; entitled *Copy-right Law,* it was published in London in 1903. Well researched and clearly presented, it exhibits a prose style more mature and controlled than that seen in the novels. The novels became more infrequent as time passed, and it is to be assumed that when Hinkson returned to Ireland as a resident magistrate his duties allowed him little time to write. His writing, however, seems to have been an integral part of the life-style of his early marriage, and Katharine mentions with fondness the shared study filled with their respective books and manuscripts, the pleasure that the money they earned brought to them in the way of gracious living, and the social life that their mutual careers brought them.

Katharine writes at length about their life in England, their many moves and different houses and areas of England in which they lived; of their many friends and the social and literary life they led. The reader interested in the details of her long life would be advised to read her five volumes of memoirs.[46]

During nearly twenty years in England, Tynan published literally hundreds of articles, stories, novels, and collections of poetry. She was a prodigious worker and a prolific author. Writing was a pleasure to her, work to be enjoyed, and she undertook many different literary projects simultaneously. Nor did she ever allow her circumstances to interfere with her writing, whether it was ill-health or children or traveling.

She loved people and she loved company. She copied Alice Meynell in choosing to write in the midst of her family, with her children at her feet and her guests and her husband's friends filling the house with noise and friendship. Of her ability to write with conversation going on all around her she says:

I, having conquered the inability to write when a tune was being played because, living in London, I could never, never hope to escape from the barrel organs, soon learned to write under any conditions. Many women writers have assured me that my way of working would break their hearts. My deplorable facility. I would write easily or not at all; and to write not at all would be to sweep away my fabric of happiness, however little it would affect the outside world.[47]

Friends and strangers alike were amazed at her facility and her industry, and to them she would tell her not so amazing secret: "Health; regular living; no racketing; and to bed every night by eleven . . . open windows and life in the open air when it is at all possible."[48]

She loved to write out of doors. In the summer of 1897, with her babies on a blanket beside her, she wrote two novels in a pretty little coppice near their summer home.[49] In 1911 she tells us her habits remain unchanged. In that summer she wrote a novel between May 6 and June 2, and by June 13, 1911, had corrected the typescript and, she adds, still had plenty of time for her family and friends.[50]

Around 1912 Tynan and her husband decided to return to Ireland and her output, if anything, increased in the social isolation of the west of Ireland: "During my three years and a bit in Mayo I have, as a mere matter of book-making, written nine novels besides Lord Edward: A Study in Romance, which is something more than a novel; two volumes of reminiscences, three volumes of poetry, two schoolbooks, besides a great number of short stories, articles, etc. I am not specially proud of this facility of mine: it has produced a good deal of honest work, with of course, a good deal of necessary pot-boiling, and it has made some few people happy besides myself."[51]

The Hinksons had decided to return to Ireland because even after their many years in England, they still considered Ireland to be their true home, a country with which they could identify, and where they wished to spend the rest of their lives. Henry Hinkson had put his name on the waiting list for appointment as a resident magistrate in Ireland many years before, and at this time Tynan solicited the help of their friends Lord and Lady Aberdeen. Lord Aberdeen offered Hinkson the appointment in Castlebar, County Mayo, and there they returned to live until Henry's unexpected death in 1919.

Tynan found Mayo uncongenial in many ways—unfavorable weather and the lack of society—and she admits that it would have been a difficult situation for her if she had not been occupied with her writing. Isolated as she was, she was far removed from the political upheavals in Dublin in 1916. Strangely, she felt more involved in the war effort which involved both England and Ireland from 1914 to 1918, and much of her writing at this time was devoted to war poetry and memorial articles for magazines and newspapers. Her children had been at boarding schools in England, but in time her sons were to join the English forces fighting in Europe and her daughter was to return to live with her parents in Mayo. Those were busy years for Tynan and years of anguish and worry concerning the fate of her sons and the sons of her friends. It was with great relief that she greeted the end of the war and their return home. Another sorrow was to greet her in the following year with the death of her husband. She writes in *Memories* that "Grief had come to me at the end of the War as though the immunity of the boys had been bought with their father's life."[52]

This sad time she leaves in obscurity, although she does write with a rare bitterness about her circumstances after he died.[53] The resident magistracy in Ireland was a job which demanded much from the holder in the form of subsidizing the expenses incurred in the carrying out of the job. A holdover from the days of patronage, it paid little, and, on her husband's death, Katharine discovered that the job, though a government post, provided no pension for the survivors. Consequently, she was left in straitened circumstances. She was a widow at the age of fifty-eight and was to survive her husband by twelve years, during which time she was to continue to support herself and earn her own living by writing.

She and her daughter traveled in those years, and their travels are described in Tynan's two books, *The Wandering Years* (1922) and *Life in the Occupied Area* (1925). She spent much of her time in England and occasionally lived for stretches of time in Dublin. They were indeed years of wandering, unexpected and unlooked for, and yet she rose to the occasion as she had throughout her life. She continued her prodigious output of novels and poetry until the end of her life; she continued to enjoy traveling, her many friends, and her beloved children and grandchild.

After a long life full of the joys and sadnesses of living and loving, Katharine Tynan Hinkson died in London in 1931 at the age of seventy. She was buried in London beside her friend Alice Meynell, whose husband Wilfred had helped launch Tynan's career and from whose house she was married many years before. She lies not far from the grave of Francis Thompson, her much admired fellow religious poet. The day before her funeral the British Broadcasting Company broadcast on radio the following poem written during Tynan's exile in England, years when she longed for the country and company most dear to her:

At Euston Station

Yon is the train I used to take
In the good days of yore,
When I went home for love's dear sake,
I who go home no more.

The station lights flare in the wind,
The night is blurred with rain,
And there was someone, old and kind,
Who will not come again.

Oh, that's an Irish voice I hear,
And that's an Irish face,
And these will come when dawn is near
To the beloved place.

And these will see when day is grey
And lightest winds are still
The long coast-line by Dublin Bay
With exquisite hill on hill.

I would not follow if I might,
Who came so oft of old;
No window-pane holds me a light,
The warm hearth-fire is cold.

There is the train I used to take.
Be blest from shore to shore,
O land of love and of heart-break!
But I go home no more.[54]

CHAPTER 2

First Fruits

A poet's or novelist's first book is always of importance, first to himself, and second to the critics who hope to ascertain its literary worth. Katharine Tynan's first book, published when she was in her early twenties, was both a financial and a social success. It took the reviewers by storm in a way that the modern reader can hardly understand. The major newspapers and journals in England and Ireland greeted it with acclaim and praise far exceeding its intrinsic worth, and, as a consequence, she was considered in Ireland the most promising young poet of her generation. She was not to lose this place in public esteem until the arrival on the literary scene of a greater genius, W. B. Yeats.

I First Book of Poetry

There were few poets of equal ability writing at that time as prolific as Katharine Tynan and fewer still had a published book to their names. *Louise de la Valliere and Other Poems* (1885), seen through the press by Wilfred Meynell and subsidized by her father's money, saw print in the easiest possible way.[1] Already well known through her contributions to English and Irish journals, Katharine's reputation as a rising new star was confirmed by her first book. Its success opened up limitless possibilities for future publishing and future literary contacts. At the age of twenty-four Katharine Tynan was an established poet. This new status was to have both beneficial and detrimental effects on her poetry and on her career.

The slim volume opens with the title poem "Louise de la Valliere." A lengthy dramatic monologue written in quatrains, it deals with the romantic story of Louise's life and retirement to a convent in eighteenth-century France. It is a romantic young girl's poem, and it is easy to see why the subject would have appealed to Tynan, imbued as it is with suppressed physical passion, a dark gothic atmosphere, hints of sin and the decadent life of the rich, and the heroine's valiant and successful efforts to repent and defeat her temptation in the night corridors of her convent. The poem would have slight appeal to the modern reader, not so much because of its theme, but because of the obscurity of reference, and its use of archaic language which Tynan at this time considered poetic. The formal usage of "Thy" and "Thine" and the archaic endings of the verbs which she uses throughout are jarring. The poem is full of color, but this overusage of both adjectives and adverbs likewise would have fitted her early unsophisticated definition of the poetic. The theme, tone, and diction are illustrated in this passage which tells of Louise's troubled past:

> Surely, these things had brought me full content,
> Were I Louise clear-eyed and innocent,
> Fifteen unsullied summers 'neath the skies.
> I am Louise, sinner and penitent.
>
> Ah! the child's heart o'erfull with trust and joy!
> Lord! it grew world-sore, stained with earth's alloy;
> Till one came smiling by, and taking it,
> Broke it as children break a worn-out toy.
>
> Even this poor heart Thou, Lord, didst not refuse.
> Long Thou didst wait as one that knocks and sues
> At a heart's door that opes not to admit,
> While on his gold locks fall dank night dews.

This long poem is immediately followed by an ode entitled "The Dreamers." This, too, shows the weakness of her style in the repetitive use of apostrophe, e.g., "O Feet," "O Dreamers," "My birds." Again, her diction is archaic in her use of words such as "yea," in a mock biblical style, and in the use of the apostrophe to indicate dropped or missing letters as in the line "I' the heart of shade." There is no need in most cases for the dropping of the consonants, but all of these features were to Tynan proper poetic form and language.

The volume as a whole indicates her preoccupations in her early twenties when she was living the life of a girl in her father's house at Whitehall. There are a number of nature poems: "A Song of Summer," "A Bird's Song," and "Poppies" among them. These are aptly entitled songs and are brief and, for the most part, pretty descriptions and observations of nature. It is evident in the early nature poetry of her career that her love for birds, trees, flower and field was deep, spontaneous, and full of energy and genuine joy. The poems succeed in that they convey this energy and joy to the reader. Tynan seldom draws parallels with life or points a moral in these nature poems, and, consequently they remain fresh and delicate.

An even greater number of poems in this volume deal with religion. The religious element of the title poem has been mentioned. The long poem "Joan of Arc" recounts the young Joan's thoughts in her prison on the morning of her execution. Written in rhyming couplets the poem has a genuine poetic strength in its energy, easy flow, and vignettes of Joan's life as she recalls the various events of her past. It is spoiled by its diction, but, if this is overlooked, the poem can serve to illustrate Tynan's narrative ability in verse and her maturity in the handling of her subject.

This poem and "Faint-Hearted," "Vivia Perpetua in Prison," "The Dead Christ," and "A Tired Heart" all deal explicitly with Catholic religious themes. A number of these are addressed, like prayers, to the Lord, to Christ, and talk in personal terms of the poet's relationship with God. These poems are filled with conventional Christian imagery, and the language does little to lift them into the realm of good religious poetry. They evince an attitude of total trust on the part of the poet toward God. There is no room in her devotional verse for the slightest expression of doubt, the merest question of belief or unbelief, the least despair or fear. Her childlike faith remains unshaken. At the age of twenty-four, it must be admitted, her life experience had been such that her firmly rooted Catholic faith had yet to be challenged. She continued to believe what she had been taught. When in later life she was confronted with profoundly tragic experiences her faith was to change but only to become deeper. It will become apparent in this chronological study of her poetry that she was never to take or to consider alternatives, and, as a result, her religious poetry remains relatively static throughout her long career.

In the religious poems in this volume Tynan addresses God or Christ with the understanding of the deity in its anthropomorphic shape. She perceived Christ more in human than in divine terms, but she remained unconcerned with theological issues, mystical experience, or in the development of the soul. Her interest resided in man as a creature relating to his God, not so much in the form of his Creator but in the idea of Christ, the Redeemer, the sharer in our common humanity.

Deriving from this initial conception of Christ as our brother in the flesh who suffered, lived, and died, came Tynan's ideas of the saints, in particular, Mary, the mother of Christ, and St. Francis of Assisi. The portrayal of Mary is notably absent in this particular volume because Tynan had yet to experience those events—marriage, motherhood, loss—that would bring her into a closer relationship with the idea of Mary. Closer to her own wishes and dreams at the age of twenty-four was the independent, unconventional young girl from the country who wore men's clothes and lived for a while in a man's world of war and bloodshed, the innocent maid who went to her death so courageously. She saw in Joan of Arc someone with whom to identify, for Tynan, too, was a farm girl, sheltered, innocent, who hoped to write, to succeed in what was a male-dominated profession. Joan could have provided her with a noble and inspiring role model at this stage in her life. A passage from the poem makes this possibility clear:

> . . . On yonder pallet lies,
> For the morrow's shows, my woman's draperies.
> And now, fair armour, that hath held me fast
> In all my great, glad days, gone with the past,
> I lay you down—my knightly days are o'er—
> The coming dawn sees me a maid once more.
> Indeed, for France I gave my womanhood,
> Nor knew the foolish, sweet thoughts that are food
> Of other maids, the love that one brief day
> Painteth with pearl and rose the canvas grey
> Where their small lives are limned; and yet this heart
> Beats woman-tender, though I stand apart,
> Knowing not joys that other women know—
> The lover's love, the mother's joy and woe;
> And I have taken ofttimes and caressed,
> For some dumb yearning stirring in my breast,

> A peasant's babe, and laid its clinging arm
> On my mailed neck, and kissed it close and warm,
> So that it thought the mother held it still,
> The little tender, sweet thing, and had will
> To lie in dumb content, like a bird i' the nest.
> But I am happier, singled from the rest
> To do Thy will. . . .

The poem "Fra Angelico at Fiesole," although dealing with the Italian monk and painter, Giovanni de Fiesole (1387-1455), is not a religious poem. The first stanza tells of the surroundings in which he lived and what his observant and artistic eye perceived:

> Home through the pleasant olive woods at even
> He sees the patient milk-white oxen go;
> Without his lattice doves wheel to and fro,
> A great moon climbs the wan green fields of heaven.

The poem is beautiful in its simple rhythm, absence of archaic diction, and easy rhyme. Its every line is filled with color and imagery, but the poem can bear the profusion because of its simple statement. Such color and imagery are evident in the last lines which describe the spirits that visit the painter's studio:

> They kiss with fair pale lips the canvas wide,
> Whereon his colours like dropped jewels glow
> Against a gold ground pale as the harvest moon.

This poem shows the influence, although faint, of Robert Browning's poetry, in its subject matter, and, possibly, in the abundance of its description. "My Lady: A Portrait" shows some influence of Browning as well in its approach to its subject. Throughout the volume, particularly in the title poem and in "King Cophetua's Queen," Tennyson's influences can be seen in Tynan's choice of subject and theme.

Contemporary critics saw in the volume the major influence of the Pre-Raphaelites, in particular, the Rossettis. Tynan, however, refutes this: "I never saw Rossetti's *Poems* before 1884, when I was visiting in England, and as most of the poems gathered into *Louise de la Valliere* were written in the early eighties, the influence from Rossetti which the critics found in the little book must have travelled to me somehow on the air. Perhaps there is more of a real influence from him in the later verses. I certainly did write some very Rossettian verses after I read him, but I don't think they got into print."[2]

Although Tynan had not read Rossetti, the influence of the Pre-Raphaelites permeated other works by poets, writers, and artists which were available to her. What is important is the fact that Tynan does not trace any direct influence to Rossetti. Before her meeting with W. B. Yeats, Tynan was not subject to any direct poetic influences but to general influences of various Irish and English traditions. Her formal education had been sporadic and undisciplined. Her reading, particularly of poetry, was broad and unselective. She read, as she admits, everything that came to hand. The propaganda poetry of the earlier Irish writers was always available to her in her father's house. The major conventions of English poetry filtered through to her in her reading of anthologies. Her knowledge of current trends came to her in fits and starts depending on what magazines and newspapers were available to her in the small library she frequented. She certainly possessed a natural facility for writing poetry, and her inclination had led her early to verse making, but isolated as she was, in a way, in her room at Whitehall, her intellectual grasp of poetic theory and history was weak. Her taste was untutored and her likes all-embracing. While she read literally everything that came to hand, she was unable, alone, to discriminate, and her approach to poetry remained emotional rather than intellectual. Poems appealed to her because of their theme in most cases and not because of their language or structure. In the early days of their acquaintance Yeats was to tease her because she valued Shelley and Longfellow equally, and she admits it was not until his comment that she began to see the poets in perspective according to their ability.[3]

II   The Irish Voice

Despite Tynan's isolation from an intellectual community at this time in her early life, despite the often deleterious effects of her reading, and the influence of a confluence of numerous poetic traditions, both Irish and English, and long before her association with Yeats, Hyde, and Russell, she was struggling to find her own poetic voice. That she composed and offered in her first volume three poems which were notably Irish in theme is proof that she was not merely a follower in Yeats' footsteps, a handmaiden to his ideas on the writing of poetry. She made a move in her own poetry which paralleled Yeats' efforts in his poetry, but which at this early stage was not influenced by him.

The first of these significant poems was entitled "The Flight of the Wild Geese," footnoted for the benefit of the English readers. The "wild geese" of the title are those Irish men who left Ireland after their defeat by the English and the subsequent Treaty of Limerick.[4] The phrase is not Tynan's but one which had been current in Ireland for decades. She takes the phrase and develops the image of geese, of birds flying far from the Ireland which needed them. Apart from its theme, a single reference to Patrick Sarsfield, the Irish hero, and the reference in the last line to "blessed Irish ground," the poem's language, diction, and imagery are fairly universal. "The Dead Patriot" deals with a returned exile, A. M. Sullivan, a patriot who died in 1884. The Irish reference in this poem lies in the image of the shamrocks which pillow Sullivan's dying head.

Both these poems follow in the tradition established in the early nineteenth century by Thomas Davis' *The Spirit of The Nation*.[5] It was a tradition which encouraged the writing and publishing of poetry which was political rather than artistic in its aims and purposes. Davis was a patriot whose purpose was to arouse a defeated people and set their heroes and their just causes before their eyes in an effort to inspire them to nationalistic fervor and action. Indifferent to the literary qualities of the writing, he inadvertently established a tradition which was followed for half a century by the young writers of Ireland. When they wrote of Ireland they were inclined by the tradition to write of political wrongs, military and political heroes, exiles and their tragic deaths, or passionate longings to return to mother Ireland. This is the poetry of lament, grief, and sentimentality; it is also often the poetry of propaganda, hatred, and incitement. There did exist alternative models—not all Irish poetry in English was so narrow in its aims or poor in its quality. James Clarence Mangan, Sir Samuel Ferguson, and William Allingham did indeed write poetry which was Irish in subject matter, theme or imagery, and reference, which however avoided the pitfalls of propaganda. Theirs were the true voices of poetry in English in Ireland in the nineteenth century and their poetry provided Yeats with an alternative tradition. Tynan had yet to discover the value of these poets, and it was Yeats, as she admitted, who pointed the way out of the maze of the *Nation* poetry to the goal of a truly national poetry. However, without yet having come to terms with the powerful poetry of Mangan and Ferguson, she did produce one poem at this time, the third Irish poem in the volume, which showed more than any of the others, the promise of her talent.

The poem is entitled "Waiting," and the footnote to the poem adequately sums up its story line: "This poem treats of a legend well known among the peasantry of the north of Ireland which recounts how a band of Irish warriors of the primeval time lie in armour, and frozen in a deathly sleep, in one of the hill caverns of the Donegal highlands, there to await the hour of Ireland's redemption, when they will come forth to do battle for her under the leadership of the giant Finn. . . ."[6]

Compared with the other poems in this volume, this poem shows a great advance in Tynan's style, control of language, and, most especially, choice and treatment of subject matter. The slow steady rhythms and the simple diction joined to some truly impressive images give an impression of Keats' influence on this poem in particular.

The poem is weighty in imagination as in theme: it opens with the following two stanzas which illustrate Tynan's dramatic sense, visual imagery, and control of rhythm:

> In a grey cave, where comes no glimpse of sky,
> Set in the blue hill's heart full many a mile,
> Having the dripping stone for a canopy,
> Missing the wind's laugh and the good sun's smile,
> I, Fionn, with all my sleeping warriors lie.

The delayed introduction of the subject of the sentence, the personal pronoun, until the fifth line is a marvelously controlled device to capture the interest of the reader and gain full effect in the stateliness and emphasis of the phrase, "I, Fionn."

The next stanza has echoes of Keats' *Endymion:*

> In the great outer cave our horses are,
> Carved of grey stone, with heads erect, amazed,

> Purple their trappings, gold each bolt and bar,
> One fore foot poised, the quivering thin ears raised;
> Methinks they scent the battle from afar.

Fionn, the speaker, goes on to describe his hound, well known in Irish legend, Bran, "deep throated . . . mighty flanked and fleet." He describes himself, his warriors, and their queens, and explains why they wait in deathless sleep. He recounts what he has seen as his "eyes look with a solemn gaze of woe/From stony lids adown the centuries." He viewed from his cave the advent of Christianity and the life and death of Christ. Tynan resists the temptation to elaborate on this theme and restrains the verse so that the reaction of Fionn and his men, ancient pagans, is presented as being full of wonderment, mystery, and interest. On the day Christ died, Fionn tells the reader:

> Then I upraised myself with mighty strain.
> In the gloom, I heard the tumult rage without,
> I saw those large dead faces glimmer plain,
> The life just stirred within them and went out
> And I fell back, and grew to stone again.

He recounts the events of the passing of time; how he had heard of the various wars and battles down through the ages. He is trapped, helpless, until that one final battle when he and his men will be called from their stony sleep. And so they wait:

> Once in my time, it chanced a peasant hind
> Strayed into this cave. I heard, and burst my chain,
> And raised my awful face stone-dead and blind,
> Cried, "Is it time?" and so fell back again,
> I heard his wild cry borne adown the wind.

While they wait, others wait, dead princes buried in foreign lands with their faces turned toward Ireland, for the day of the final battle.

It is an impressive poem in its own right, but even more impressive when seen in the context of the whole volume. This poem illustrates Tynan's real ability, her genuine talent when she restrained her impulse to sentimentalize. The poem has dignity, stateliness of rhythm, restraint, and carefully chosen diction; an intriguing story line which is presented with brevity, compression, and an eye to the dramatic effect. The images are well chosen and well developed. Importantly, this poem is the only one in the volume which deals with time and which indicates that Tynan had some sense of the past and its relation to the present. Compared to her other dramatic or narrative poems which are seldom rooted in time, except in the superficial awareness of dress or speech, this poem clearly indicates even in its title the poet's understanding of the powerful theme of the transiency of life and the intransiency of time.

It is surprising that this poem was not included by Tynan in her various collections or in the two modern collections of her poetry. "Waiting" is the best poem in Tynan's uneven first volume. Together with "Fra Angelico at Fiesole," it gives the reader an understanding of her potential at the age of twenty-four. The poems show maturity of treatment, controlled style, a fine eye for detail and image, and an interest in two major themes of poetry: time and art. These two very different poems also indicate the range of her ability. "Waiting" would have been sufficient in 1885 to place her in the first rank of the young Irish poets. It and the poems in *Shamrocks* put her side by side with Yeats and Douglas Hyde as the forerunners of the Irish literary revival.

In summary, Tynan's first book, *Louise de la Valliere,* was important not only to herself but to the incipient Irish literary movement. Paid for by her father, it entered the world untried by any editorial criticism or competition for publication. It was greeted enthusiastically in both England and Ireland, in a manner far beyond her own expectations or indeed the merits of the poetry itself. But the critics had praised and the public had bought a new name, a fresh and spontaneous imagination, poetry of delicate and sincere feelings and simple themes. What remains to the modern reader with the proverbial hindsight are a small number of poems of real merit, one of which identifies her firmly as an Irish poet. Apart from this evidence of her ability, the book stands as an important historical document in the evaluation of the early history of the Irish literary movement.

III   Tynan's First Prose Book

Tynan's first prose book had an equal impact on her career as a writer, even if it did not have as important an effect on the incipient Irish literary movement. The work was commissioned by the Irish nuns of the Loreto order. It had the improbably long title: *A Nun, Her Friends and her Order: Being a Sketch of the Life of Mother Mary Xaveria Fallon (Sometime Superior General of the Institute of the Blessed Virgin in Ireland and Its Dependencies).* Published in 1891, the book is dedicated to Wilfred and Alice Meynell.

Tynan was the natural choice for the writing of this biographical sketch. As the most popular and famous Irish Catholic poet of her day, known for her simple piety and strong faith, she would have come to the attention of the nuns. Moreover, as a woman attuned to the life of Catholic women, and as a former student in a convent school, she was familiar with, and certainly favorable toward, the life within convent walls. Yeats saw the writing of the book as a "momentous matter" and "was greatly pleased," commmenting that her "prose is often so very good that it may be quite a notable book."[7] He also saw it as the possible "beginning of a new literary life."[8] And indeed it was, because it started her on a career as a novelist that was to continue for the next forty years. Yeats could not have foreseen the direction her writing would take in the coming years, for in a way this book was a turning point in her career that was to take her away from their original and shared goals. The book proved to Tynan that she had a facility for clear, flowing prose. She wrote the book easily and quickly, and it found a small but ready market because her reputation had preceded her. She now began to consider enlarging her career goals to include the writing of fiction as well as poetry, the kind of fiction she wrote easily and which sold quickly.

This first book, however, is of little interest today. It is stiff in both style and language, but this is because of the subject matter with which Tynan had to deal. She was constrained by both the expectations of the nuns and the conditions inherent in writing a book of this kind. With her subject and audience constantly in mind she adapts her language, and her prose takes on a tone of polite formality, dignity, and sometimes strained stateliness, as in the following passage: ". . . meanwhile she was praying and serving, now mounting noisome garret stairs with her beautiful sister, the twain bringing food. . . ."[9]

The book was adequate for its purpose and pleased those who commissioned it, but to the modern reader the biography does not exhibit any real warmth. It is far more interesting for Tynan's portrayal of the appealing aspects of convent life and her particular preoccupations: one with the innocence of the nuns and their childlike manner of speech and behavior; the other with the theme of the pain a mother must endure when giving her child to God in the life of the convent. These themes and her pen sketches of the pastimes of the nuns recur innumerable times in her later novels.

For example, early in the book she writes: "Every nun looks like a Madonna and the Madonna is the exemplar to more than Irish Catholics of all that is lovely and pure in feminine nature. The nuns make the girls ladies, if that is at all possible, for every nun is a lady, and the standard of refinement in convent and convent-school life is, if anything, excessive."[10] Tynan knew whereof she wrote, since she herself had attended just such a school, and her own sister Mary had hoped to enter a convent before her untimely death.

In a statement that reveals her own feelings and explains her subsequent preoccupation with the figure of Mary, Christ's mother, in her poetry, she writes: "Mary, Mother of God, is the ideal set before all Catholic women. From their childhood they are taught to weigh their action by her modesty and humility and patience."[11] That Tynan did just that is evident in her religious poetry, especially after her marriage and the deaths of her first two children.

The book received favorable reviews in *The Irish Monthly* which praised her for her great diligence, discretion, and literary skill. The *Athenaeum*, the *Manchester Guardian*, and other English journals were also favorable in their comments, pointing to the great appeal of her graceful, dainty sketches of the nuns and their lives. The book received greater attention than is usual for this type of biography because of Tynan's recognition as a poet. However, the book also received considerable adverse criticism which she herself explains in *Middle Years:* "When I began writing I had been hailed by the priests as the new young Catholic poet. The priests had sent my first little volume of poems into edition after edition, to the bewilderment of my publisher, Mr. Kegan Paul, who used to say that mine was the only poetry that sold with him . . . my Parnellism meant my being cast out . . . almost as a heretic, a schismatic."[12]

She also tells us that she was doing remarkably well in her career in 1891, "considering that I had not yet published a volume of prose, excepting my *Life of a Nun,* which had been torn to rags and tatters by the Anti-Parnellite organ, the National Press, to the great distress of the poor nuns for whom this biography of one of their number had been written."[13]

The Parnellism which Tynan mentions in these passages refers to her devotion and adherence to the ideals of the Irishman Charles Stewart Parnell. Because of Tynan's public role as a new young poet, her sympathies with Parnell and his goals became well known and consequently the book, and, indeed, her poetry, were criticized on the basis of her political stance and not on their literary merits.

Charles Stewart Parnell, born in 1846, in County Wicklow was the outstanding political figure in Ireland in the 1880s. Son of a wealthy landowner, he was a member of the Protestant Anglo-Irish ascendancy in Dublin. Educated at Cambridge University, he returned to Ireland to work unceasingly on behalf of the people. Elected as a member of Parliament from County Meath, he eventually became the leader of the Irish members in the English Parliament who were seeking home rule. Home rule, which would have meant an Irish Parliament sitting in Dublin, distinct from the Parliament in London, but retaining its ties with the British Empire, was seen by many, including Parnell, to be the first officially sanctioned, legal, and substantial step on the road for complete independence for Ireland.

A brilliant, strikingly handsome man, he was tremendously popular with the Irish people for whom he labored. As he moved closer to success in his agitation for home rule his liaison with a married woman was made public. To summarize a complex issue very briefly, the priests who had been in the forefront of his supporters in Ireland turned against Parnell because of what they perceived as his unacceptable behavior and bad example. His political organization was splintered and the movement defeated. Parnell, weakened by imprisonment, ill health, mental strain, and fatigue died shortly thereafter in 1891.

Tynan admired Parnell and had worked with his sister in the Ladies Land League.[14] She shared in Yeats's admiration and enthusiasm for the man, and both defended him in their different ways and were outspoken and valiant in that defense. A split developed in the society of Tynan's day, and, as she records, for many years following Parnell's death people continued to identify themselves as Parnellite or anti-Parnellite, and violent partisan argument caused many ruptures in her large circle of friends. Her own position became well known in Dublin and in England through her literary contacts, and she became an object of some criticism because of her Parnellite sympathies. She became unpopular for a time with that audience that had perceived her as first, a Catholic writer, and only secondarily as an Irish writer.

Tynan's approach to politics at this time and throughout her life was unsophisticated and emotional. Parnell as a figure had captured her imagination in much the same way as the historical figure of Lord Edward Fitzgerald was to do in her later life. Her devotion to these figures was that of a young girl for a romantic aristocrat, the fallen hero, brought down, in Parnell's case, by ignorance and hypocrisy. She favored Parnell's policy of home rule, but came to disapprove of the Land League movement of which he was also head at one time, because of its violence, and because it was attempting to shatter the old order which depended on the society of the wealthy landowners.

Tynan had few political opinions; she had a weak understanding of historical movements in Ireland or in any other country, no interest in political theory of any kind, and, after her initial involvement in the Ladies Land League which she saw as mainly social, she did not involve herself in any real political activity. In her early life she had absorbed a patriotic love for Ireland from her father which provided fertile ground for the influence of John O'Leary, Yeats, and Hyde and other members of her circle who were the new young breed of nationalists. In her formative years she had read about a gracious way of life in the novels available to her, and her father made every effort to create a similar kind of life-style in their home at Whitehall. She was accustomed to servants being at hand and to the presence of laborers and retainers on her father's property and lands, and she grew used to the feeling of, if not the substance of, real wealth and the advantages it endowed. Throughout her twenties she attempted to approximate the leisured style of life of that class which was immediately above her own in the stratified Irish society of that era.

Neither born nor bred into that upper class, she still attempted to acquire its external attributes. She was not interested in wealth but in that type of life which wealth could provide in the late nineteenth century, a life of ease, refinement, leisure, good food, good company, vacations, and the absence of any physical labor. Spoiled, in a sense, by her own father's generosity and overt favoritism, she looked for the rest of her life for the kind of life he had provided for her. It is obvious from her autobiographical works which cover this period in her life that the fame and social importance which her role as successful writer brought to her were substantially more important to her than her art.

As a result of her initial and favorable experiences in her twenties, her tastes were formed for life. Consquently, she wished the world, her particular world, to remain as it had been when she was young. She viewed the essentially feudal society of nineteenth-century Ireland in the best possible light. It was an ordered world to her mind, one with an educated, rich and established upper class maintained by the majority, the lower class. It was a world in which everyone knew his or her place and was happy in that place. As a writer and poet, Tynan was considered an artist, a member of that intelligentsia which formed, not a class of its own, but a body of people that was aligned to the upper class, a group which could appreciate and enjoy the finer things of life, aspire to social position regardless of background, and achieve entry into that world of the aristocracy. She looked at her world not through rose-tinted spectacles but with blinders on her eyes. By nature a personality who tended to look for good in everyone and everything she encountered, she saw only good in the way of life which appealed to her. She never looked beneath the ordered society which existed before the Great War, and never accepted in the years following the war that the ordered society, that genteel world, was lost forever. She lived the remainder of her life seeking it out in her own way and recreating it in her postwar novels.

It is too simple to explain Tynan's political thinking by describing her as a snob. She was always engaged with the individual, never the group, and, lacking the historical sense, she extended her judgments of individuals to the groups to which they belonged. The ascendancy in Ireland was fine because the members of it whom she knew personally were fine and cultured people, gracious and generous. The poor of the Dublin streets were happy because the ragamuffin newsboys from whom Tynan bought her papers were always smiling and jovial. It can be suggested, too, that her Catholicism gave her a measure of tolerance of the status quo. Her Catholic teaching would have impressed upon her the great importance of acceptance, the active accepting of God's will. This strain in her thinking is obvious in the poetry she wrote concerning those tragic events in her own life. It is not too much to assume that her early exposure to such a philosophy predisposed her to take the world as it was and then to get on with the living of her own life.

CHAPTER 3

Tynan, Yeats, and the Irish Literary Revival

THE Irish literary revival or Irish Renaissance, as it is sometimes called, is a convenient phrase for indicating the change that took place in Irish literary life and thinking in the 1880s and 1890s and which was spearheaded by W. B. Yeats. Briefly, this was a movement which sought to move away from the propagandistic poetry of the *Nation* poets, the Young Irelanders, and to return to the authentic themes to be found in the Celtic history and legends, in the peasant tales and superstitions, and in the history of Ireland found in both folklore and ancient literature in translation from the Irish language. Yeats saw that the old myths, tales, and legends, almost untapped at this time, would provide an unending and fruitful source of material for the poets: plots for narratives, images for lyrics, new ways and manners of expressing themselves that would be authentically Irish and not merely inherited from the English poetic tradition. He hoped this body of material would stimulate the Irish in the same way as the Greek and Roman myths and history had stimulated the English poets of the romantic period.

Tynan, while naturally following in the predominant English tradition, was liberated by her own discovery of the power of Irish legend and eventually by Yeats' advice and influence. What brought Tynan and Yeats together in terms of literature was their mutual recognition of the inadequacies of the poetic traditions which were available to them—both English and Irish. Tynan's approach to the writing of the new Irish poetry seems more intuitive when compared to Yeats' intellectual grasp of the situation. Nevertheless, though coming by different routes, they reached the same conclusion. This chapter examines Tynan's role in the early days of the literary revival.

I   *Tynan's Meeting with Yeats*

Previous to the publication of Tynan's first book of poetry she had published a number of poems in the *Irish Monthly,* and became acquainted with Father Russell who was to remain her friend throughout his life and who was mentor to many young Irish writers of the period.[1] Through her publications Tynan also came to the attention of the young Charles Hubert Oldham of Trinity College, Dublin, who was attempting to start what became the *Dublin University Review,* a serious literary magazine, unconnected with but named for Oldham's university. Oldham requested her help by asking her to contribute a poem because, not only was she a young Irish poet but, more importantly, a poet of established reputation. She agreed to help, as she continued to agree, throughout her career, to help young writers who sought her advice. Oldham had met the young William Butler Yeats and his father, John Butler Yeats, and had already agreed to publish Yeats' lengthy early poem, "The Island of Statues." Oldham showed this poem to Katharine Tynan and eventually brought Yeats to call on her at Whitehall; Yeats was twenty and Tynan twenty-four when they met.[2] The relationship which grew from that first meeting in 1885 was to become significant to both of them in a number of ways.

In the early days of their relationship the friendship was both personal and literary. It reached its deepest intensity on both levels during the years preceding her marriage and thereafter dwindled as their lives and work took very different directions. She writes extensively about Yeats and their friendship in both *Twenty Five Years* (1913), and *Middle Years* (1916). Her picture of Yeats, written many years after he had become an established poet of first rank and a public figure in Ireland, retains the freshness of Tynan's first impressions of him as a young man. She paints an intimate portrait of a man much written about, and her reminiscences are characteristic of her personality.

Older than Yeats and generally maternal in her relationships with men, she saw him as a tall, lanky boy "all dreams and gentleness." Her picture of him was one that he approved: "He was beautiful to look at with his dark face, its touch of vivid colouring, the night-black hair, the eager dark eyes . . . and he lived, breathed, ate, drank, and slept poetry."[3] It is a romantic but personal portrait of the young Yeats, borne out by photographs and pictures of him from this period.

She admits that she bullied Yeats because in her practical way she did not want to live entirely for poetry.[4] She wanted to live sociably and enjoy the friendships, excitement, adventure, and fame that being a young established female writer offered her. She at all times acknowledges his genius and his influence, and she claims rightly that she perceived it in him in those very early days. However, her self-reported treatment of the beautiful dark genius was gently mocking, affectionate, and prodding. Impressed by his personality and his talent, she nevertheless was for some time in control of their relationship.

Through her friendship with Yeats, Tynan was introduced into the circle of his remarkable family. She became an intimate of J. B. Yeats' Dublin studio which was visited by notable writers, artists, and thinkers, its atmosphere dependent on the dynamic personality of the portrait painter, a brilliant conversationalist. In the summer of 1886, J. B. Yeats painted Tynan's portrait which was exhibited at the Royal Hibernian Academy exhibition of 1887.[5] Her description of the studio during her sittings indicates how she valued this opportunity to mingle with and listen to the members of Dublin's avante-garde. Such early exposure to the life of the artist and the intellectual helped to prepare her for the many literary friendships which she would maintain later in her life. She writes:

I used to come in about eleven or twelve o'clock in the morning and sit till lunch time. At various moments in the morning the Yeats girls and Willie would arrive, one at a time; and during the sitting there was a continuous stream of visitors. Mr. Yeats never found any visitor or any amount of talking a distraction from his work. His visitors, perhaps, were only the right kind, or it may have been that they were made right by his extraordinary interest in his kind. He did not dislike many people. Those I have heard him express dislike of were generally the peevish, unsympathetic wives of men he was fond of, who, having out-distanced him in the race for prosperity—where indeed he was never a runner—still loved excursions into Bohemia and were held back by their women folk.[6]

Through her connection with J. B. Yeats, Tynan was introduced to John O'Leary, the old Fenian who had been imprisoned, and then exiled in France for fifteen years by the

English authorities in Ireland because of his subversive political activities. He had returned to Dublin, a large impressive white-haired figure of a man who lived with his sister, a minor poet. He quickly became the focus of a group of young idealistic Irish writers. He was a genuine hero to the young W. B. Yeats from the beginning of their friendship, and he came to stand in the poet's thinking and poetry for the "Romatic Ireland, dead and gone." Tynan, too, became one of that circle for whom O'Leary's door was always open. O'Leary lent books and sometimes money to the young impoverished idealists and intellectuals and, more importantly perhaps, he encouraged them in their writing and nourished their nationalistic ideas tempered always by his own hard experience. He was kind to all, more demanding of the young men of the circle, and more indulgent and paternal toward the young women. Tynan is proud to mention his indulgent attitude and tolerance toward herself, and ingenuously reports that young Yeats at this time in their friendship (1892) "used to complain . . . that my mind had no speculation in it. I daresay I was irritatingly cocksure to one who went from speculation to speculation. John O'Leary used to throw back his old lion head and laugh and say 'Let her alone; she's all right.'"[7]

One of Yeats' "speculations" during this time was his interest in the occult. Tynan disliked these studies and experiments in the realm of the supernatural and psychic, and although Yeats, on a rare occasion, did manage to involve her in a seance, she protested. Initially, it would seem that her Roman Catholic training caused her to disavow any interest in these investigations, but in some of her remarks she explains that she had "determined to be in opposition . . . to disbelieve in it, and disapprove of it as a plaything with things of life and death."[8] She acknowledges that part of her determination not to believe resided in a real fear of the unknown and its potential, a fear inculcated in her mind by the experiences of her childhood; the wakes and funerals, the fairy and ghost stories, together with the widespread peasant superstitions available to her on her father's farm from the servants and laborers.

II   Early Days of the Revival

From the year 1885, when Yeats met Tynan, until 1887, when the Yeats family moved to London, their friendship was of mutual benefit and enjoyment. Through Yeats and John O'Leary, Tynan met many of the writers who were to form the backdrop for the Irish literary revival. She writes of the meetings with them at the O'Leary house:

> For the latter years of the Eighties we were tremendously concerned with literature and art and quite satisfied with our interests. The new Anglo-Irish school of literature was in the making. We had been discovering the way of transmuting the Irish gold and honey into the English tongue, that great and noble instrument.
> W. B. Yeats must have shown us the way, but it was surprising how easy it came when we had got the leading. We had escaped from the heartless and artificial convention which used to be set by the poets of Ireland. . . .
> . . . There was always the special circle, the O'Leary's, Rose Kavanagh, Douglas Hyde, various young men from the university, admirers and disciples of Dr. Sigerson, but always with the addition of one or two or three people from overseas.[9]

There was a fruitful meeting of minds among these young writers, an ebb and flow to their relationships which introduced fresh ideas and provided the ideal setting for the development of those ideas. Tynan's circle of friends widened to include George Russell whom she met through Yeats. Russell, who was to become known by his chosen name, A. E., was a young art student who shared ideas about poetry, art, Ireland, and the occult with Yeats. He was a gentle mystical personality with a strong practical streak. Summerfield, in his biography of Russell, writes that Tynan became intrigued with that personality: "She noticed the mixture of awkward shyness, benevolence, and genius . . . and decided that he was another Blake. Soon he was painting visionary figures for her and attending the Sunday parties at Whitehall. . . . At first he would only smile silently at these parties, but he talked to his hostess when they were alone and once told her some of the stories he had made up in his head."[10]

Tynan remained fond of George Russell throughout her life. Her memories of him are always gentle, full of love for this unworldly creative man. Russell likewise admired Tynan, especially for her religious convictions and Christian qualities. Although not bound himself by conventional religious dogma he recognized sincere religiosity, true simplicity, and a joy in life and the living of it—all of which Tynan possessed in abundance. He edited her *Collected Poems,* published in the year of her death, the volume of her verse probably most accessible to the modern reader. It is an excellent selection, representative of her best work and of that work which most appealed to him; his introduction stands as a record of their friendship and their particular perception of each other as fellow poets.

During these early years in Dublin a personal and artistic bond had also developed between Yeats and Tynan. They saw each other frequently and discussed their ideas of literature and poetry; together they envisioned a future for literature in Ireland—a vision which they shared with men such as Douglas Hyde and George Russell. In 1887, Tynan published her second book of poetry, entitled, significantly, *Shamrocks.* In that same year Yeats moved to London. From 1887 to 1893, the year of Tynan's marriage and move to England, she and Yeats maintained a steady and apparently voluminous correspondence. Although Tynan's letters to Yeats have not survived, Yeats' letters to her remain and have been published.[11] Tynan writes of Yeats' letters to her, some of which she published in her autobiographical works: "This is the youth of the poet, some years of which were mine as much as anyone's; and that they were is one of the proudest and happiest things in my life."[12]

III Shamrocks

Yeats' letters to Tynan in the year 1887 reflect the events of her career and deal in great measure with her writing and with their shared interest in the incipient literary revival. As mentioned, that same year saw the publication of her book, *Shamrocks.* That Yeats was impressed by this literary effort is seen not only in the letters but in his dedication of his own work, *Stories from Carleton,* selections from the Irish novelist, to the author of *Shamrocks.* Although Tynan's book was dedicated to William and Christina Rossetti, apparently for their interest in her first book which she had sent to them, and for their presents to her of their books and personal photographs,[13] the volume was notably "Irish" in its presentation. Bound in hard covers, deep green in color, the book's title was imprinted in gold on the cover which was adorned by small gold shamrocks in the lower right corner. Such a cover and binding were not inconsequential in those days of cheap, paperbound issues of slim volumes and small printings. The presentation of the book shows a conscious effort on Tynan's part to differentiate this second book from her first in the minds of the buying public and the reviewers. The book was published in England, and Yeats, in his letters, reflects anxiety about its forthcoming publication as if it were one of his own books.[14] In his numerous letters of this year he testifies to a shared enthusiasm for the great project of the literary revival only then just beginning and taking shape in the form of Tynan's book.

The volume opens with a lengthy narrative poem based on an Irish legend and called "The Pursuit of Diarmuid and Grainne." It is presented without notes and, as a reviewer at the time commented, it would have been difficult for the English reader and indeed the Anglo-Irish reader to understand the poem's context within the body of Irish myth and legend. However, in keeping with Yeats' admonition to find weighty and dramatic themes for their new poetry, Tynan chose a tale that is of intrinsic interest in itself, a story that shares with epic and myth a universal appeal, enhanced by, but not necessitating any Irish context. The stanzas describing Fionn, a central character, are illustrative of the poem as a whole:

> This was the bridegroom, Fionn, the King of Eire;
> Gnarled like an oak, his face like lichened stone,
> Sullen and fierce, his red eyes sunk and weary,
> Towered o'er all men that giant frame alone.
>
> Like an old tiger that hath lonely lasted
> Years after all his kin be turned to clay;
> Like a huge tree the thunderbolt hath blasted,
> Black and accursed, it stains the face of day.
>
> Yet a great hero—famed in many a story,
> Victor on many a bloody field of fight,
> But drunk with blood and war, and blind with glory,
> And, as men deemed, too old for love's delight.

The poem, written in seven sections with a rhyme scheme which Tynan had mastered, moves with easy grace and rhythm through the love story of Diarmuid, the legendary Irish hero, and Grainne, the beautiful daughter of King Cormac. It deals with the revenge of King Fionn, the man Grainne was to marry, on the young and noble Diarmuid who had eloped with her. It recounts the tale skillfully and energetically and, although the idiom is more that of Tennyson, the characters and scenic descriptions firmly root the story in Ireland.

"The Story of Aibhric" another narrative poem, is based on the legend of the children of Lir, a story also located in the body of Irish myth and legend. The story appealed to many young Irish poets, and Tynan was to use it again some years later in her poem "The Children of Lir." This narrative, not as long or as filled with action and characters as the former, depends more on description and a slow cadence which is in keeping with the sad and mournful tone of the story. Aibhric's description of himself illustrates the poem's tone and rhythm:

> Five and twenty years, and my day was at morn,
> My life at its June;
> Oh, the desolate gloaming, dark and forlorn,
> Wet skies and a waning moon!
>
> When I rode down through the reeds by the river-bed,
> Weary and faint were we—
> The good steed stumbling and hanging the noble head,
> The hounds going heavily.

The third major poem, "The Fate of King Fergus," although Irish in reference, does not match the narrative strength of "The Pursuit of Diarmuid and Grainne" nor the descriptive power of "The Story of Aibhric."

The remaining poems in the collection which are Irish in theme, reference, or dialect are "Second Sight," a lyric piece describing the magical fairy life to be found in her father's orchard, and "Shamrock Song," a poem of praise for the beloved floral emblem, symbol of Ireland over the centuries. These two and her handling of Irish legend in the three long narrative poems confirmed Tynan's role with Yeats in the incipient Irish literary revival. However, her importance rests mainly on her use of the Irish material rather than in her treatment of it. Although none of these poems move beyond the level of accomplished verse, conventional diction, and poetic forms, nonetheless, this significant number of Irish poems announced to the critics the launching of the Irish revival. The longer poems, in particular, exhibit control of the Irish material and true poetic authority in the choice of that material.

This volume contains many other poems, however, which do not deal with Irish material, and these continue to follow the thematic patterns already established in her first volume, *Louise de la Valliere*. This pattern was not to vary significantly throughout Tynan's long career, and her predominant themes are seen, even at this early stage, to be: nature; children and their relationships to the mother figure; religion, especially the Roman Catholic; and "Irish" subject matter. This categorization, although rough, provides a simple way of dealing with the hundreds of poems Tynan wrote.

Shamrocks was greeted with enthusiasm by the reviewers as fulfilling the promise of the earlier book of 1885. It contains a larger number of poems, a greater variety of subject matter, and perhaps more than any other volume, shows a more concerted effort at varying and experimenting with the structures of her poems, and more complicated meters and rhyme schemes. At this stage Tynan had yet to fall into the facile rhymes and rhythms of much of her later poetry. Among the many poems in the book, two are of special interest because of Yeats's own comments about them written at the time of their publication. His avowed favorite is the poem entitled "The Heart of a Mother."[15] It is difficult to see now why he would have chosen this poem over a number of others all rather similar. In structure and diction an extremely simple poem, it tells of a mother's anxiety about her son away at sea. The mother's constant anxiety is resolved by her son's death at sea and her imagining him safe in heaven with Christ's hand upon his hair. Yeats apparently approved of the extreme simplicity of feeling and expression to be found in this poem, something he was attempting himself in his early Irish ballads. Like George Russell, Yeats always acknowledges the sincerity and simplicity of Tynan's Catholicism, and he encouraged her to write at all times about things she knew, including her religion.

In 1887 Tynan's poetry had freshness of statement and uniqueness of treatment. Readers valued her delicate descriptions of nature which were detailed, accurate, and rendered with a loving eye. The sincerity of her nature poetry cannot be questioned in these early volumes, and her ability to condense an observation of a genuine experience of nature into a few, brief, telling lines is the very essence of lyric poetry. When her feeling for nature combihed itself with her religious sensibility, Tynan produced poems of simple and gentle beauty.

St. Francis of Assisi held a special place in Tynan's religious feeling because of his great love of nature, and his particular Christian vision of the relationship of all living things to one another as children of the one heavenly father. He is known to Catholics as that saint who most completely embodied the Christian precept of love in action. His life was one of poverty and charity. His approach was one of simple trust and faith in God and a love for all His creatures, the poor, the weak, the young—whether man or beast. The apocryphal stories of his life filled many a child's mind. His unique ability to communicate with animals of all kinds particularly appealed to Tynan, possibly because of her own great love for animals. She used many of these stories of St. Francis in her poems, and her first treatment of this subject, "St. Francis to the Birds," is found in this volume. Yeats was favorable in his criticism of these Franciscan poems and wrote to her in May of 1888:

St. Francis and the Wolf is beautiful—most beautiful—it is one of your very best, it has all the beauties of your new manner, like St. Francis to the Birds. My father, and indeed we all are, is delighted with it. It is so temperate and naive and simple. Like St. Francis to the Birds, it has a peculiar kind of tenderness, which I think comes from your religion, I suppose, yet I do not find it in other Catholic poetry. Even in your poetry, I think, it has only come this last year or so.[16]

IV   The Poems and Ballads of Young Ireland

Yeats' letters to Tynan were full of encouragement, advice and mutual planning. In that same year 1888 the little circle centered at the O'Leary's undertook a joint publication of a small book of poetry. This slender paperback, entitled *The Poems and Ballads of Young Ireland,* is the subject of many of Yeats' letters and, no doubt, Tynan's to him in London. She was Yeats' primary contact and main correspondent during this time, and, through her, he kept in touch with the activities, poetic and otherwise, of the group in Dublin. The book was published in 1888 and contained among others certain poems by both Yeats and Tynan. Yeats used the occasion of the writing of these Irish poems for joint publication to push home his literary objectives.

He tells her in the summer of 1887 to remember that "by being as Irish as you can, you will be more original and true to yourself and in the long run more interesting, even to your English readers."[17] In an earlier letter he wrote that he felt more and more "we shall have a school of Irish poetry—founded on Irish myth and history—a neo-romantic movement."[18].

Tynan wrote three poems for the little book that was to announce this new movement to the literary world. The first of these entitled "The Grave of Michael Dwyer" is a long poem of twenty stanzas, using a simple rhyme scheme and a basic ballad four-beat line. The poem's strength lies in its broken rhythms, and a number of striking images culminating in the impressive final stanza:

> And now I weave of my idle fancies
> All for the love of you,
> A wreath of passion-flowers and pansies
> Twined with Shamrock and bitter rue,
> To lie on the grave I never knew.

In keeping with Yeats' dictum, she had indeed turned to Irish history for her subject matter. Her choice of subject is of more interest, indeed, than the poetry she wrote about it. Tynan did not possess, as can be seen in her early Irish narrative poems, a true sense of what could be accomplished by the enlightened selection of either workable myth or historic figure of interest to the reader at large. In this case, of the many Irish figures available to her, she chose Michael Dwyer, an Irish hero certainly, but a pragmatic and practical man whose real nature does not shine through Tynan's romantic verses. Born in 1772, he joined the United Irishmen and took part in the disastrous rising of 1798. He escaped capture and lived for five years in the mountains outside Dublin, inspiring the English forces to build a military road into Wicklow for the sole purpose of his capture. He assisted in the preparation for Emmet's abortive rising in 1803, and hearing of its failure, remained with his men in the mountains. However, he eventually surrendered on condition of his being transported with his family to the United States. The

English reneged and sent him instead to their penal colony in Australia where he died many years later. In retrospect, his life was not such as to inspire the hero worship of Tynan's poem. It would seem that her choice was governed by the long tradition of poetry already available in Ireland which dealt with the fortunes of exiles and the tragic fate that forced men to leave their native land and live abroad. There was a long history of emigration, both voluntary and forced, in Ireland's annals, and it was a common theme for the sentimental poetry of earlier poets, and a tradition from which Yeats had broken and was encouraging others to abandon.

Her next poem in the volume is entitled "Shameen Dhu" and is of interest because it is a story told in, what Tynan thought to be, Irish dialect. We know from others that she herself had a strong country accent, different from the educated or city accent. The Irish dialect was available to her from those people she knew well on her father's farms and the surrounding villages. She writes in this vein, for example, the following lines: "Avic, the long road wasn't long/Whin we thravelled it together. . . ." The poem is written entirely in this kind of language. Yeats himself attempted at this stage in his career the same kind of language, using tortured spellings to transcribe the accent and capture the pronunciation of the Irish peasant.

Writing—poetry, drama, and fiction—which made use of dialect was part of the overall nationalist purposes of the Irish literary movement. Tynan's use of dialect in her poetry is weaker than her use of it in passages in her novels where language is wedded to character and enhances her portrayal of rural Irish people. Yeats' use of dialect in his poetry was likewise weak until he met Lady Augusta Gregory with whom he seriously studied the dialect of the people who lived in and around her estate at Coole, County Galway. Douglas Hyde's use of dialect struck the note of authenticity because he, unlike Tynan and Yeats, had mastered the Irish language, the grammar, rhythm, and pronunciation of which influenced the English language as it was spoken in rural Ireland. John Millington Synge, a young Irish linguist, advised by Yeats to leave Paris to learn Irish in the Aran Islands off Galway, became the unquestioned master of dialect. His plays, written on Irish themes in authentic speech, mark the high point of this aspect of the nationalist movement in Irish literature.

Tynan's dialect poem again deals with a forced exile. In this case, the speaker in the poem tells of a happy young man who could sing and lilt with the best. He is evicted from his small farm by the landlord and, although he is in love with a girl of property, he is too proud to live off her land and too poor to ask her to come away with him. He departs, she dies of a broken heart, and no one in the village ever hears from him again. The speaker of the poem prays for him that he keep his heart and soul true to the girl, whether alive or dead, and that he keep his lovely voice as well. The poor quality of the verse and the weak narrative sense do nothing to lift this poem out of the sentimental and the banal. The plot, however, was to become a favorite with Tynan, and she was to use it again in her novels and sketches.

The final poem she wrote for this volume is of more interest because of its unusual subject matter. Despite her strong Catholic faith and simplistic religious convictions, Tynan was very broad-minded and tolerant, for one of her background and education, concerning the subject of relations between Protestant and Catholic in Ireland. This aspect of her thinking has more scope in her later novels, but this poem is, perhaps, the first instance of her treatment of the theme in a public manner.

The poem in question, "Papist and Puritan," is the only poem in the book that acknowledges the religious divisions that existed in Ireland at that time; the only one to point to the existence of the Anglo-Irish living in Ireland since the days of Oliver Cromwell. Tynan's poem rightly points out the fact that these families loved Ireland as much as the native Irish Catholic population in some cases. In this poem the man is a Puritan, a Protestant, of an old Anglo-Irish family. The girl he loves is a Papist or Catholic. "Her creed is holy" because it is hers and he loves her. He will marry for love, despite the advice of his minister, and there the poem ends. Although the poem does not offer a solution to the very real obstacles in the way of mixed marriage in Ireland, it is, nonetheless, testimony to Tynan's recognition of the realities of religious and political life in Ireland and to her convictions, gently and persuasively presented.

Tynan knew many Protestants and non-Catholics in her circle of acquaintances in Dublin, among them Yeats, Russell, and Hyde. These relationships no doubt had a broadening influence on her thinking. It is to be remembered, too, in this connection, that her own grandmother had married a Protestant and broken with her family in order to do so. This and her own father's broad spirit of tolerance, combined with her fortuitous friendships with many non-Catholics and intellectuals, served her well. She was able in her work and in her life to escape the narrowness common to her class and religion in Ireland, and she eventually married Henry Hinkson, himself a Protestant.

Tynan's tolerance and her simple religious piety were valued by Yeats. So, too, was her warm personality. The letters of 1888 reveal a very lonely young Yeats living in London. In the winter of 1888 he writes to her: "It is pleasant to think that this will go away out of this horrid London and get to the fields and rattle along in the basket with the letters from Clondalkin to Whitehall—I wish I could fold myself up and go in it."[19]

Their relationship, however, was maintained within the rigorous conventions of Victorian behavior. It is in a letter of October, 1889, that he addressed her still as "My dear Miss Tynan" and adds in parentheses "I wonder if it would matter if I put your Christian name. . . ."[20] And he concludes one letter of the same period with the lines: "Write to me. Write to me. Write to me."[21]

In letters of this same period Yeats also talks about his hopes that the two of them will publish a ballad book of their own, commenting that she was not at her best in her poems in the earlier ballad book.[22] These letters are also indicative of the value he placed on her praise and criticism of his own work.

By 1891 the relationship as shown in the letters was beginning to change subtly and slowly. In the letters which survive there is no mention of Yeats' involvement with Miss Gonne nor his proposal of marriage to her. And in a letter of July, 1891, he refers to a boy called Hinkson, obviously in response to a question from Katharine Tynan, and he says that he did not know Hinkson at the school which they both attended.[23] It is Yeats' only reference to the man Tynan was to marry in 1893.

V   Ballads and Lyrics

The year 1891 was to see the publication of Tynan's *Ballads and Lyrics,* the last of this trio of her first and most significant books of poetry. Yeats greeted it with enthusiasm, writing to her in December to tell her how fine he thought the poems were, claiming "They are quite your best work. The 'Apologia' is exquisite."[24] The large number of poems in this volume cover the broadest range of subject matter she had attempted to deal with up to this date.

This volume contains Tynan's most popular and well-known poem, "Sheep and Lambs." It stands in relation to her own work as Yeats' "The Lake Isle of Innisfree." Neither poet considered the individual poem to be among his or her best work. Each regretted the overwhelming popularity with the public of the two poems. As Tynan's most famous work, the poem is worth quoting in its entirety:

> All in the April evening,
> April airs were abroad,
> The sheep with their little lambs
> Passed me by on the road.
>
> The sheep with their little lambs
> Passed me by on the road;
> All in the April evening
> I thought on the Lamb of God.
>
> The lambs were weary, and crying
> With a weak, human cry.
> I thought on the Lamb of God
> Going meekly to die.
>
> Up in the blue blue mountains
> Dewy pastures are sweet
> Rest for the little bodies,
> Rest for the little feet.
>
> But for the Lamb of God,
> Up on the hill-top green,
> Only a cross of shame
> Two stark crosses between.
>
> All in the April evening,
> April airs were abroad,
> I saw the sheep with their lambs,
> And thought on the Lamb of God.

The appeal of "Sheep and Lambs" rests in the simplicity of its imagery, of its diction, and in the succinct reference to the Lamb of God who is Christ. The poem is markedly different from the mass of her devotional poetry because of its brevity and the delicacy of her style. Often heavy-handed in her religious imagery, often overstating the private intensity of her religious beliefs, much of her inspirational poetry borders on the sentimental. However, she achieves a marvelous poetic restraint in this starkly simple poem written out of an actual experience, just lightly touching on the religious meaning and significance by putting the two images in conjunction: the actual and the spiritual, leaving the reader like the poet herself, to think on the Lamb of God. This poem was eventually put to music by Sir Hugh Roberton and retains today its popularity as the choral work "All in the April Evening." As a result, Tynan's delicate little poem and her name are known to many who otherwise might not have encountered her work.

"A Led Flock" in the same volume attempts a similar simplicity, but Tynan's single image is strained: the waves of the sea are a flock kept by the Lord and the Lord speaks, saying that the mother of drowned sons would view the waves of His sea as an angel of life, not of death, because of the great happiness her sons found in the afterlife. In comparison with the previous poem it fails significantly. These two poems illustrate by contrast the unevenness of her poetic sensibility because of her inability to choose workable images with consistency or authority. The theme of St. Francis and his communion with the natural world is treated again in "Of St. Francis and the Ass" and in "St. Francis: His Wrath" but both are weakened by sentimentality, conventionality of rhyme and imagery and, as a result, do not compare with her earlier poem on the same theme.

"All in All" is a reflective poem, a prayer, and the precursor of many prayers in Tynan's corpus. Addressed to Christ, the poem admits of Tynan's failings and weaknesses and her aching to be purged of guilt and woe. The poems written in this mode are seldom revealing of any particular weakness or sin, or any internal struggle in a matter of faith or morals. The poet does not concern herself with matters of theology or philosophy. Her religious poems are always spontaneous, the simple cry of the common man to his God. As a result, her religious poems offer little to the more sophisticated reader or the reader who does not share her convictions, but offer much to the reader who, believing, can accept in her poetry such total simplicity of faith and trust.

The honesty in this poem and the many like it reveals nothing of her religious personality, and suggests that she never encountered a crisis of faith, or struggled intellectually or emotionally with her God. At its best her religious poetry with its simplicity of statement, language, and image is pure, stark, and memorable. However, it remains within the genre of poetry written by her friends Alice Meynell and Louise Imogen Guiney, poetry which did not attempt to attain the imaginative power, spiritual beauty, and strength of the poetry of her other close friends Francis Thompson and Lionel Johnson, in whom she recognized a special gift.

The volume also has a profusion of nature and bird poems for which Tynan had a real talent. Adept at selecting lovely images with an eye for true, telling, delicate detail, she also possessed the gift of compression so necessary for lyric poetry: an ability to describe briefly and beautifully her observations and impressions. Among the loveliest are "A New Old Song," with its extremely effective end rhymes and sprightly rhythms conveying a sense of spring; "Winter Evening," with its cloud imagery, and "Storm-Gold," which tells of the beautiful peace and calm which follows both the natural storm and the storms wrought in the heart by love.

Few of the lyrics in this volume speak as directly as Tynan's later poems concerning events in her personal life. "Moods," however, does tell of the effect of the wind, as it blows from south or east, on her disposition. "The Blackbird" suggests a personal element in its little story wherein the blackbird is her love with whom she wishes to build her nest. Unlike the poems Tynan wrote later about her father, the poems which deal with her love for her husband and their married life always make use of a private language of birds and flowers through which she speaks, using images from nature to parallel the actuality of human events and personalities.

"Lux In Tenebris," however, speaks directly of her lifelong fear of the darkness of the night, and it is one of the loveliest of her many prayers:

> At night what things will stalk abroad,
> What veiled shapes, and eyes of dread!
> With phantoms in a lonely road
> And visions of the dead.

The kindly room when day is here,
At night takes ghostly terrors on;
And every shadow hath its fear,
And every wind its moan.

Lord Jesus, Day-Star of the world,
Rise Thou, and bid this dark depart,
And all the east, a rose uncurled,
Glow golden at the heart!

Lord, in the watches of the night,
Keep thou my soul! a trembling thing
As any moth that in daylight
Will spread a rainbow wing.

A large portion of the poems in this volume are Irish in theme or subject matter. They include a number of ballads which make use of folktales of the fairy world, folklore, and stories. Among these are: "The Fairy Babe," "The Death Watch," and "The Fairy Foster-Mother." "The Witch" is a fine ethnic poem with great energy and wit. Its songlike rhythm and rhyming couplets inspire the reader to read it aloud. A poem exhibiting a sense of fun, it is blunt and colloquial with an interesting little plot concerning a churn of butter charmed to turn sour by a neighbor. The spell is lifted by a fairy man, a man gifted with secret power and the knowledge of twigs, plants, and herbs.

There are also a number of ballads written in the traditional mode of the Irish lament. "The Wild Geese: A Lament for the Irish Jacobites" takes up its theme from earlier nationalistic poetry. A song in structure and language, it mourns for all kinds of Irish heroes and is an unremarkable effort in its genre. "The Charity of the Countess Kathleen" is one of the early treatments of this story translated from the French which was to capture Yeats' imagination, in particular, and one of his first plays was to handle the same material. The ballad tells the story of the wealthy Kathleen who was loving and generous to her people. In the dark days of the famine she had done everything possible to alleviate their suffering, spending her fortune to procure food. As the story goes, two agents of Satan were sent to buy souls of the starving people with food or money. Grieved by this, Kathleen offers her own pure and devout soul in an exchange for the souls of her people. The agents, realizing that to capture such a prize is worth the other souls together, strike the bargain. God, however, intervenes and rescues Kathleen's soul from the consequences of the bargain.

"The Children of Lir" is another poem of which Yeats approved. With a swinging rhythm and vivid, detailed natural description, the ten stanzas tell the story of the four children of King Lir who were "glamoured," an Irishism for bewitched, by their stepmother. Hugh, Fiachra, Conn, and their sister, Fionnuala, have been turned into swans. Because they have retained their human characteristics of intelligence, memory, and communication, their lives as birds are weary, lonely, and frustrating. They have no hope of escape from their situation, and they wander, sad and hopeless, on the streams and lakes.

Tynan sets the scene in the first two stanzas in which she creates the somber atmosphere that fills the remainder of the poem. The first stanza is an example of her poetic power at this stage of her career:

> Out upon the sand-dunes thrive the coarse long grasses,
> Herons standing knee-deep in the brackish pool,
> Over head the sunset fire and flame amasses,
> And the moon to eastward rises pale and cool;
> Rose and green around her, silver-grey and pearly,
> Chequered with the black rooks flying home to bed;
> For, to wake at daybreak, birds must couch them early,
> And the day's a long one since the dawn was red.

Tynan had learned from her familiarity with Irish ballads the effective use of the refrain. In the three stanzas in which the children recall their memories of their happy human life, filled with hurling and ballplay, banquets in the great hall, human love, and companionship, Tynan ends each with the touching refrain, spoken by Fionnuala: " 'Peace,' saith Fionnuala, 'that was long ago.' " The final stanza closes on the scene with which the poem opens, and, in its delicate tints and shading and its gentle rhythm, creates the strong impression of the loneliness of the Irish landscape which lent itself, in part, to the development of these ancient legends:

> Dews are in the clear air, and the roselight paling,
> Over sands and sedges shines the evening star,
> And the moon's disc lonely high in heaven is sailing,

Silvered all the spear-heads of the rushes are,—
Housed warm are all things as the night grows colder,
Water-fowl and sky-fowl dreamless in the nest;
But the swans go drifting, drooping wing and shoulder
Cleaving the still water where the fishes are.

"The Children of Lir" is one of the best examples of the heights Tynan was able to reach during this particular phase of her career. It illustrates the fine work which she could achieve when her particular talents for vivid description, detailed observation, and the rendering of touching human emotions were wedded to an intrinsically interesting, manageable, and authentic Irish source which was as yet fresh and untapped.

Because of the ability demonstrated in poems such as "The Children of Lir," Yeats, both at the time of their friendship and later, continued to consider Tynan his first and equal partner in his endeavors to renew and revitalize Irish writing. She herself modestly gives Yeats the entire credit. In *Twenty Five Years*, she writes:

We were terribly unexacting with ourselves in those days. We were appallingly easily satisfied with our achievements, as were our friends and critics. . . . I myself have been compared to Sappho and St. Teresa in a breath. I have, moreover, been called a fine flower of womanhood, and a divinely gifted daughter of the gods. . . .

. . . To return to Willie Yeats and the movement with which he had more to do than anyone else. In fact, he was "The onlie begetter" of the new Irish poetry. Heaven knows what rubbish he delivered us from! We were all writing like the poets of a country newspaper, copying a simplicity of the older poets which had long ceased to be simple, aiming at a rhetorical passion which had never been sincere.[25]

VI   *The Continuing Relationship*

During the early years of her poetic career which corresponded with their friendship, Tynan paid heed to Yeats' advice. In 1888 he writes to her: "Your recent poems have been beautiful, any you send me, so full of calm and temperance as well as the old qualities of energy and beauty. I think you will be right to make your ballad Irish, you will be so much more original—one should have a specialty. . . . You have yours in Ireland and your religion."[26] At the end of that same year, he writes to her again of her need for a specialty, one that was ready to hand in her case. In the same letter he points to both her strengths and her weaknesses:

Your best work—and no woman poet of the time has done better—is always where you express your own affectionate nature or your religious feelings, either directly or indirectly in some legend; your worst, that which stands in your way with the best readers, where you allow your sense of colour to run away with you and make you merely a poet of the picturesque.

To soften the blow of this criticism he includes his own poetry in his criticism, both contrasting and comparing it with her own:

The want of your poetry is, I think, the want also of my own. We both of us need to substitute more and more the landscapes of nature for the landscapes of art. I myself have another and kindred need—to substitute the feeling and longings of nature for those of art. The other change—a less important one—you perhaps need most. It is curious— do forgive me all this—that your other fault, that of sometimes a little overstating the emotion, is only present when your landscapes are those of art. We should make poems on the familiar landscapes we love not the strange and glittering scenes we wonder at; these latter are the landscapes of art, the range of nature.[27]

She did indeed follow this very specific advice, and a glance at the progression of her volumes of poetry shows her shifting away from medieval and eighteenth-century themes, Tennysonian structures, and epic stories to the narrower field of subjects which she knew well: nature in all its detail of flower and tree; simple religious feeling rooted in her understanding of St. Francis and Christ; Irish myth and story with which she became familiar at Yeats' recommendation.

In the spring of 1889 Yeats suggests to her that the two of them undertake another book of ballads and this suggestion, although the book was never to come about, indicates that he considered her to be the appropriate partner in such an enterprise.[28] Yeats had a keen and businesslike appreciation of the market available to them and how it could be appealed to for the benefit of those young writers in Ireland, and, of course, himself and Tynan. He hopes that the literary critics will perceive them to be a new school of Celtic poetry, because this would provide publicity and inspire interest in the buying public.[29] He urges on her the need for a book about Irish writers and their lives and works: "It would sell largely, I hope, and do good work I am sure. Some day you or I must take it in hand. There is a great want for a just verdict on these men and their use of Ireland."[30]

Yeats, in keeping with his long-range plans for the literary revival, believed that the Irish poets and writers of his generation should work with Ireland and her future literature always in mind. He early saw the pitfalls of facile journalism and easy money both for himself and others. He saw danger in it for Tynan, and recognized that her facility in writing sketches and interviews, short and superficial pieces for ready money, could well lead her talent astray. He recognized that her easy and unrevised prose—an ability he had not mastered—could lead to a lack of discipline. At the end of 1889 he wrote to her on this very subject that was beginning to turn her talent away from their heretofore mutual goals.

When you write, always tell me what you are writing, especially what poems, the journalism interests me more dimly of course, being good for many people, but no way, unless on Irish matters, good work for you or me, unless so far as it be really forced on us by crazy circumstances. At least I think this way about it, not with any notion of poets' dignity, of course, but because so much in the way of writing is needed for Irish purposes. You know all this as well as I do, however. Much may depend in the future on Ireland now developing writers who know how to formulate on clear expressions the vague feeling now abroad—to formulate them for Ireland's not for England's use. Well! One could run on endlessly in this kind of way and you who love men and women more than thoughts would always grow indignant.[31]

Although Tynan was often to follow Yeats' advice in the matter and manner of her poetry, turning to the simple ballad form as he recommended, turning away from English literature and English traditions in her early poetic career, she was not to follow his advice in this matter of journalism. She had begun on a prolific career in journalistic writing in which she began to spread her talent too thin for its strength.

Perhaps, unsure of her poetic gift, she turned readily to prose, and her easy facility in prose was to prove the beginning of the end of her literary partnership with Yeats. She writes with satisfaction of her prose writing in direct contrast to Yeats' stated opinions:

My old life was by this time coming to an end and the new life in view. I had a prodigiously industrious winter and spring . . . writing all manner of things, increasing my already large correspondence forever striking out in new directions, writing in new places, making new friends. I was writing for the *Speaker,* the *National Observer,* the *British Weekly, Good Words,* the *Magazine of Art, Atalanta,* the *Woman's World* (of which Oscar Wilde was editor) *Sylvia* . . . besides my American, Catholic and Irish papers and magazines.[32]

At this stage of her career Tynan was immature in her poetic thinking and inclined, as Yeats saw, to a sociability which was in stark contrast to his own ideas, at that time, of the poet as a solitary personality. Reinforced by too much praise too early in her poetic career, and excited by success both financial and social, she did not recognize the seriousness behind his admonition. In a review of another Irish poet, John O'Donnell, Yeats makes clear his disaffection for the kind of writing in which she was now engaged:

With more leisure or more culture, O'Donnell might have discovered a style quite his own. As it was, he was stifled by journalism. "Talking of work," he wrote in 1872, "since Sunday, two columns of notes, two columns of London gossip, and a leader, one column, and two columns of verse for The Nation. For Catholic Opinion, two pages of notes and a leader. For Illustrated Magazine three poems and five columns of story." A style is not picked up in this fashion. A career of this kind for a man of imagination, if voluntary, is a crime; if involuntary the greatest of misfortunes; and yet O'Donnell seems to have been rather proud of it. "I write verse faster than prose," he said. Oh thou great abyss of inane facility, how many fine natures hast thou swallowed—above all, how many Celtic ones. An unkind Providence has granted to us Irish folk a terrible love of immediate results, wholly fatal to great work.[33]

The parallels between O'Donnell's work and his approach to it and Tynan's writings and her attitudes toward them are obvious. Her name and her own statement previously quoted could easily be substituted for O'Donnell's in Yeats' review, and Yeats' criticism would as surely apply to her facility. He saw such journalism as a crime if undertaken voluntarily, and, at this time, Tynan undertook it voluntarily. Later it would become an important part of the family income, but in these early days before her marriage and before financial necessity governed most of her choices in writing and publishing, she still had the freedom to choose the greater disicipline of art. She chose, however, the immediate result.

Despite Yeats' disappointment in the way her career was taking shape, the correspondence between them remained vigorous until her marriage and move to England, where they saw much of each other in the early days of her marriage. She remained during those pre-England years his most faithful correspondent, his personal friend, who shared mutual friends and literary contacts in Ireland, who kept him informed not only of her own activities but those of their friends. She reviewed his work favorably in the press, and took part in various projects and literary societies whenever possible. In her poetry she was to continue until middle age to follow his advice, to write of Irish subjects, to continue to consider herself as Irish even during her many years of living in England. Even when she eventually abandoned the ideals he had instilled in her in terms of her own writing, she continued to take an active interest not only in his work but in the work of her contemporary Irish writers and the new generation following them. She corresponded with Irish poets, and made efforts in various ways to put before an English audience the work of those Irish writers in her *Cabinet of Irish Literature* and in the various collections which she edited.

Yeats, in turn, continued to credit her with a major role in the Irish literary revival and to take a continuing interest in her poetry. In 1895, two years after her marriage he was still able to write to her: "Now that Christina Rossetti is dead you have no woman rival. You, Ferguson and Allingham are, I think, the Irish poets who have done the largest quantity of fine work."[34] This is great praise from the poet who was to outshine them all, and speaks of Yeats' continuing hope that Tynan would adhere to their youthful and mutual poetic ideals and shared ambitions.

After 1895, their paths, once parallel, began to diverge, slowly at first, and then, eventually, more rapidly. Tynan's marriage and the subsequent deaths of her first two infant children disrupted the close personal relationship that had existed between herself and Yeats, and put an effective end to her underlying maternal attitude toward the young Yeats. Home, family, practical necessities began to occupy her more, while, at the same time, Yeats was entering a turbulent period in his creative and emotional life which was to center effectively around Miss Gonne for some years to come. With the change in Tynan's own writing career, and with Yeats' increasing interest in the theater, the gap between them eventually widened.

Significantly Tynan's last volume of poetry, *Irish Poems* (1913), which retained in some measure her earlier commitment to Irish themes and subjects, called forth a response from Yeats many years after their friendship had cooled. The interest and attention are still there but his critical opinion of her work is tempered. He sees clearly where her own personality and the circumstances of her life have brought her poetic career. His estimation of her ability is fair and stands today as his summary statement on the poet who had embarked with him on a momentous literary movement: "I think you are at your best when you write as a mother and when you remember your old home and the Dublin mountains. The first of the .two poems should be in all the little ballad books,—if there will be any more little ballad books—alas—now that we—you and I chiefly—have made a change and brought into fashion in Ireland a less artless music."[35]

There is a certain sense of sadness and nostalgia in these lines. Fair to the end in his critical estimation of her work he sees how far she has strayed from her early promise and potential. He sees now, in 1913, that she writes as a mother and an exile, but he still shares with her in this private letter as he did in his public statements, the credit for the change wrought in modern Irish writing. He saw Tynan as a good minor poet who had produced work of lasting value. Her talent was outdistanced by his genius, but it was a sure talent, and she is remembered today for being that which he always believed her: an equal partner in a warm personal relationship and a fruitful, cooperative, creative endeavor. Once considered to be the most promising young Irish poet until the arrival of Yeats on the scene, she, as Yeats himself perceived, would have held pride of place with Allingham and Ferguson as the leading poets of the nineteenth century.

Tynan however, in her own reminiscences about Yeats and their friendship, takes no such credit. In her opinion it was Yeats who "showed us the way." And her memories of their relationship focus on the personal rather than the literary aspect. Concluding her chapters dealing with Yeats, she writes in *Twenty Five Years:*

My desire has been to show what a poet, who has more than fulfilled all that was expected of him, was like in his eager and fervid boyhood. I think the letters present a charming personality, and it is a cause of great pride with me that I was so closely associated in friendship with the writer of the letters at a period when his work was just beginning. I feel that I have a bit of him which no one else has, in his simple and touching boyhood. It is curious to find myself engaged in the attempt to humanise "Fairy Willie" as a friend of mine calls him. What courage! What presumption! I think he was human enough and very lovable. I wonder how I bullied him and drove him all over the place as I did. The ignorance, the hardness, the self-satisfaction of youth! But at least he derived happiness from the friendship—that is plain enough in the letters; and doubtless he understood, perhaps even liked the bullying.

Remembering the poems he has not written, I close this page of W. B. Yeats with a malediction upon the Irish Theatre, which could have dispensed quite well with the sacrifice of what was given for the supreme delight of mankind.[36]

Theirs was a fascinating friendship, and the record of it in her memoirs and his letters sheds light on the deeply human side of two poets whose relationship, and the fruits of it, would change the course of Irish writing; on the times in which they lived and wrote; on the earliest beginnings of that Irish Renaissance.

CHAPTER 4

Tynan's Poetry: The Middle Period

IN 1893 Katharine Tynan married Henry Hinkson and moved to England where she would live for the next twenty years. Her creativity was not interrupted by these significant changes in her personal life and *Cuckoo Songs*, her next book of poetry, appeared in 1894. Five hundred copies were printed for the English market and the book was dedicated to her husband. The title page is illustrated with a woman in classical pose holding a three-stringed instrument which suggests an image of the Irish harp which recurs throughout her writings. In *The Wild Harp*, a selection of poetry which she edited in 1913, she writes explicitly of this image. "The harp does not laugh, it does not think, it does not teach. The Irish harp had three strings, the old poets said long ago. The first string sang of youth, love and the joy of battle; the second of grief and death; the third of forgetting and sleep—and the third was the sweetest string of all."[1] These harp-strings correspond with the types of music the ancient Irish *Ollamh* or musicians had to master: "geantraighe"—the strain evoking laughter; "goltraighe"—the strain inducing tears; "suantraighe"—the slumber bringing strain.[2]

I   Cuckoo Songs

The thirty-three poems in this volume cover a broad range of subjects, and the choice is in keeping with the three general divisions as indicated by the three strings of the harp. However, the poems vary considerably in quality, owing to her inability to distinguish her good poems from her weaker ones.

The volume opens with a miracle play in verse, entitled "The Resurrection." A long poem written in a didactic tone, it is a weak beginning to the book. The theme as presented in the epilogue is the strength of women: a woman bore Christ; a woman was the last person at the foot of the cross on which He died; a woman was first to the tomb on Easter morning. Mary is presented as a model for all women, and Tynan, as poet, admonishes women to "Be virtuous wives and housekeepers;/ Keeping the home as sweet as Hers./The first of happy home-builders." The epilogue introduces a theme that recurs in all of her writings from this time on. The theme remains consistent throughout and, dating from the time of her own marriage, deals with her perception of the role of woman as wife and eventually mother. Besides this religious verse play there are a number of inspirational poems in this volume, all pleasant, simple, sometimes sentimental little pieces.

Poems in this collection which deal with Irish subject matter or are Irish in treatment continue to place Tynan at the forefront of the Irish literary movement in company with Yeats. Among these are "The Oak Said to the Eagle"—a poem from the Irish language; a variation of the traditional Irish story of the red-haired man's wife; and a strong lament, written in dialect, entitled "An Island Fisherman." "Colleen Rue," a love song, and "The Dawning of the Day," a strong unsentimental piece, are both Irish in reference. The poem called "Ivy of Ireland" acknowledges her continued allegiance to Parnell but is a rhetorical work that does not do justice to her deep feelings for the Irish political hero. Eight of the total number of poems can be considered as Irish poems and form a substantial part of the book.

There are also a number of nature poems using bird imagery in particular, and, although most of these are merely pretty works, the poem "God's Bird" is strong and interesting.

Finally, there are a number of poems which obliquely reveal her feelings at this time of her marriage. "Pot Pourri" is one of the earliest poems in which Tynan speaks with sweet remembrance of the month of May. She was married in May, and the many poems she writes about marriage invariably refer to the special happiness she associated with that particular month. "The Only Daughter," a strongly rhythmic poem, tells of a girl who loves her sad and lonely father but who still leaves him to go with her lover. Considering the date at which she wrote this narrative poem, it may be regarded as autobiographical. It is also possible to see a personal reference in the "Wood Dove" which employs a sprightly rhythm and in which the poet identifies with the dove. The simple refrain "true love is enough" reflects the happiness she herself found in her marriage. Another poem which refers to marital bliss is "Ceann Donn Deelish" ("dear brown head") and the extra line in the final stanza of this poem is extremely effective.

In summary, *Cuckoo Songs* is a substantial but not an outstanding book in Tynan's corpus. It continues the categories which she had established earlier: nature poems, religious or inspirational verse, poems which are Irish in reference or mode, and love lyrics. The major contribution to her reputation lies in the Irish poems; the personal interest in those lyrics which reveal her own feelings.

II   A Lover's Breast-Knot

The volume which followed, published in London in 1896, is almost entirely rooted in her own feelings and experiences. *A Lover's Breast-Knot* is a collection of lyrics which, through nature imagery, in particular that of flowers, speaks of the joys and sadness of her early married life. The book is dedicated to Harry (her husband) who is called by the name. of the flower, heartsease. The first eighteen poems are love poems, and their subjects are obvious from their titles, for example, "Love's Trouble," "Love's Flight," "Love Impatient," etc. The poems are intensely personal and often touching in their simplicity of expression, frankness of sentiment, and honesty of emotion. Read together they tell a story which Tynan refrained to speak of in her many autobiographical works. Using the nature imagery extensively enabled her to displace her feelings, to distance herself by projecting those feelings onto birds, symbolizing emotions by using the traditional language of flowers—a language which would have been more readily understood by readers of poetry at the turn of the century than now. One clue as to why Tynan is so noticeably silent about her husband and their relationship in her prose writings can be found in the poem "Love's Praises." In this poem, the narrator is presented in conversation with other women who are talking of their lovers and their feelings for them. She, however, cannot speak of her love, cannot praise him in company, cannot tell of her feelings because they are so deep, so secret, and finally so intense, that "silence and tears beseem them best." Following these collected poems Tynan was rarely to write about her husband in her poetry.

These poems are testimony to both the physical and spiritual sides of Tynan's love for her husband, and some are memorable because of their intensity and honesty. In "The Lark in Love," the lark is presented as minstrel, lover, and bridegroom at once together, just as Tynan saw her husband in relation to herself. In "Love's Trouble" she prays for protection for him while he is abroad in the world. In "Great Love" she states clearly that only divine love could exceed the love she bears for him, and she commends him to it if she should die. In "Love's Watchfulness," a less dramatic poem, her love is seen to be warm, simple, protective. The image she uses, where she sleeps if he sleeps and she wakes if he wakes, hints at the comfort she found in their physical relationship in marriage.

One poem in this section fully reveals the sense of security and self-worth which marriage gave to Tynan and which she continued to see as one of the most important benefits of married life. In "Love's Carefulness" she writes of that curious change that love can effect in the personality: she has come to love herself because her lover loves her. Of the remaining poems in this section, a number are weakened by her loss of control over the nature, bird, and flower imagery which swamps the lyrics and obscures the meaning. However, one of the best nature poems Tynan was to write is included in this section and is entitled "August Weather," the fourth lyric in the series "Love's Summer." It is a fine example of her poetic power, observant eye and artistic control:

> Dead heat and windless air,
> And silence over all;
> Never a leaf astir,
> But the ripe apples fall;
> Plums are purple-red,
> Pears amber and brown;
> *Thud!* in the garden-bed
> Ripe apples fall down.
>
> Air like a cider-press
> With the bruised apples' scent;
> Low whistles express
> Some sleepy bird's content;
> Still world and windless sky,
> A mist of heat o'er all;
> Peace like a lullaby,
> And the ripe apples fall.

The second section of the book is dedicated to Godfrey, Tynan's first child who died in infancy. None of these poems succeeds as poetry because, perhaps, the emotion is too raw, and the author seems unable to transmute the emotion into art. The tone of the poems is one of deep sadness, and the purpose of many of them is to console herself that the child is in heaven where she will one day see him again. However, the spiritual consolation of these poems pales beside the physical imagery which she uses. In "The Sheepfold" she tells of a ewe which has lost its lamb, and how the milk meant for that lamb runs out from the sheep like tears. The sense of physical loss and waste is poignant. In "Garden Secrets" the emotion is again displaced onto nature and speaks of "Our ruined nest in the tree." Tynan often equated her various homes with nests and the meaning behind the poem is clear. In "The Child in Heaven." she acknowledges that the refrain she uses in the poem is taken from another source. That she uses it herself indicates how apt she found the image to be. The poem tells of a childless mother who finally, in heaven, finds a child to love and nurse: the refrain which tells how she will "Kiss his brows and his lips apart/And give him milk from her lonely breast" needs no explication.

III   The Wind in the Trees

Tynan's life was full of sadness in the years 1894 through 1896. She was to lose another child in infancy and to move away finally from the cottage in which she had begun her marriage, full of happiness and confidence in life and all that it held in store. There is a lapse of some two years before she brought out another book of poetry, entitled *The Wind in the Trees: A Book of Country Verse* (1898). Dedicated to Alice Meynell, the book contains poems previously published in magazines and papers.

The book opens with poems dealing with January and ends with poems about Christmas. Primarily nature poems, they follow the cycles of nature and the seasons of the year. Throughout there is recurrent use of bird and flower imagery, with some mention of her longing for Ireland, and four poems about lost babies. Of the collection, two stand out: one, entitled "Drought," that is powerful in its sensory imagery; the other called "Sparrow," a short piece about the clever city bird that visits the country to refresh himself, "But holds that still the town is best/For men and birds of wit and taste."

The book is important in that it marks a change in Tynan's poetry, a retreat away from the areas of interest and exploration that had occupied her: the Irish subject matter that had established her central role in the revival; the deeply personal lyrics of loss and love; even the religious and inspirational verse she wrote so easily. The reader senses a retrenchment on Tynan's part, a distancing of herself from her poetry. Loving poetry for its own sake, she continued to write but finds, perhaps, relief in writing about the objective natural world she had always loved. Possibly the cyclical nature of the work reflects her own hope and trust in the cyclical nature of her own life and marks, in this fallow period, the wish to submerge herself in nature, its returning seasons, its rhythms, and its promise.

IV   Poems

Her next volume, published in 1901, exhibits a further distancing of her poetry. The dedication to the Right Honourable George Wyndham, M.P., chief secretary for Ireland and descendant of Lord Edward Fitzgerald, marks a change from the personalized dedications of Tynan's earlier volumes. She had much admired the efforts of this English statesman on behalf of the Irish people. Her dedication of her book to him was a public statement of her appreciation of the man and his work, but it made her unpopular for a time with her more nationalistic contemporaries in Dublin.

The book, simply entitled *Poems,* is a retrospective volume of her previously published work. Tynan divides the collection into sections, grouping the poems according to the subject matter with titles such as "Country Airs" or "The Children"; or into selections taken from the previously published books: *Shamrocks, Ballads and Lyrics, Cuckoo Songs, Miracle Plays, A Lover's Breast-Knot,* and *The Wind in the Trees.* For those readers unfamiliar with Tynan's early work the book provides examples of what Katharine Tynan herself considered to be her best poetry.

V   Innocencies

After a long silence Tynan published *Innocencies* in 1905, again dedicating this volume to George Wyndham. The introductory poem to this volume states clearly the subjects and themes which Tynan was to make her own special province:

> I sing of children and of folk on wings,
> Of faith, of love, of quiet country things;
> Of death that is but lying down at night
> And waking with birds at morning light;
> And of the love of God encompassing;
> And of the seasons round from Spring to Spring;
> I sing of gardens, fields and flowers and trees:
> Therefore I call my love songs Innocencies.

Tynan was beginning to narrow her field of endeavor in poetry throughout the early years of the twentieth century. This volume shows a limiting of her range of subjects to those mentioned in her poem: birds, children, nature, death, faith, and love. Her treatment of these subjects likewise reflects a narrowing of her attempts at different meters and structures. At this time Tynan chose simple forms which she was able to handle with felicity and ease. Uncomplicated structures and obvious rhyme schemes with steady four- or five-beat lines occur frequently in her poems from this time onward. The categories which she established in this book were to be maintained not only by herself but by subsequent editors of her works. Her characteristic subjects for her poetry were established now in her early middle age and reflect a more settled vision, one occupied and satisfied with the simple joys and basic beliefs of her life. Three poems in this collection illustrate this complacent vision. "Without You" can be assumed to be a poem addressed to her husband and reflects a new stability after the early sad years of their marriage. The straightforward sentiment is shown in the line: "Without You, dear, I am not comfortable." Early passion has grown into the solid comfort of companionship and trust. In "The Meeting" she describes a mother's feelings for her small child as she meets him on the stairs and the great happiness this child has brought into her life. This poem reflects the joy Tynan had in her three surviving children and in the fulfillment of her deeply maternal nature. "The Senses," a poem of thanksgiving to God, is one of the many she was to write during the middle period of her life, a time filled with security, comfort, and joy in her husband, family, and career. Her writing career was never secondary to her family life but complementary to it, the substance of her intellectual and social life as she indicates in her autobiographical writings. In this poem she acknowledges her interpretation of her writing career as a vocation, a true calling to the literary life by God. She is grateful for that calling, for the dignity of work, for both the spiritual and material aspects of that work: "I thank Him for my hands so feat/'Now write,' He said, and they have writ."

At this time Tynan begins again to write lyrics which speak of her personal life, yet these lack the candid emotion of the earlier poems in *A Lover's Breast-Knot*. In place of candor a new element of contemplation is found in her personal lyrics. Entering her middle age she has developed a reflective tone that suffuses those personal poems. Out of the tumultuous and significant events of her early career and life she has attained a new point of view: she begins to move into a new era of maturity and retrospection. Yet even these peaceful days were troubled:

Towards the end of 1906 the headaches from which I had always suffered became increasingly violent and frequent. The entries in my diary record headache and sometimes double headache which meant one headache following another—sometimes two or three days in succession. During the last fortnight of the year, seven in fourteen days—made me begin to tremble for the future of my work. . . . Francis Thompson called them hemicranial headaches because they affected one side of the head and one eye. They were in fact the true migraine, beginning with fortification figures, arcs, white flashes. . . .[3]

She was not only troubled by this physical ailment but by a rare phase of spiritual and artistic dryness. Always able to produce her light love stories for the publishers, she was not always so able or, indeed, willing to continue to write her poetry. She was filled with self-doubts at this time, perhaps more than at any other time during her career, and she explains its causes in *Middle Years:* "During the first decade of the century, dating from the time of the South African War, the poets had a bad time in England. . . . I had a period of distrust of myself and the value of what I wrote which prevented my writing much poetry."[4]

According to Tynan, by the year 1906 poetry was truly out of favor in England, and in one of her rare discussions of her own particular understanding of poetry she writes:

It was the swing of the pendulum towards material prosperity and away from spiritual things. The fluctuation of poetry as I have known it is that, we are paying the bill, as we were after the South African war, so that poetry is a thing of naught. This bill being paid, we begin to have leisure of pictures and books, so the Arts revive. In course of time we begin to be over prosperous and art becomes decadent. . . . There has to be a purging before the creative spirit arises, clean and new. If the South African war had been a bigger war I believe that it might have made poets instead of crushing poetry almost out of existence.

During those first ten years of the century, especially after we had left Ealing and the almost exclusive society of literary people, the remoteness of poetry from actual life was an overwhelming reality.[5]

Given the state of the market for poetry in England, her own discouragement and self-doubts, and her isolation from a creative milieu, it is not surprising that Tynan wrote little of significance during this period. In 1907 she attempted two very different kinds of poetry books, both aimed at the American market which she had always hoped to attract.

VI   *Books for the Market*

The first was a slim volume, *A Little Book of XXIV Carols,* published in 1907 and containing twenty-four of her spiritual or inspirational verses, including the ever-popular "Sheep and Lambs." The second book published in that year is of more interest. Covered in dark green paper and with the traditional shamrock on the title page, the book was entitled *The Rhymed Life of St. Patrick.* The foreword to the book tells of St. Patrick's vision wherein he saw the Roman Catholic faith being brought to the New World by the Irish emigrants fleeing from famine and suffering in their native country. Tynan dedicates the book to the children of St. Patrick, those Irish Catholics at home and abroad. The individual sections tell in verse the story of Patrick's life. Written in rhyming couplets, the poems exhibit weak rhyming, and the poor imagery indicates the lack of imaginative involvement in the subject on Tynan's part. The book is lavishly illustrated with black and white drawings by L. D. Symington, and Patrick is portrayed with the conventional mitre, beard, and crozier. One of the illustrations which pictures the three American cathedrals dedicated to St. Patrick clearly indicates that the book was intended to appeal to those Irish-Americans who could afford this type of gift book for their homes. The book is certainly not to be numbered with Tynan's better efforts in poetry, but it does point to her continued ambition at this difficult time and to her continued awareness of the markets which were available for her industry and ingenuity if not her talent.

VII   Experiences

Tynan began to recapture her former confidence and creativity, and she considered *Experiences,* published in 1908, to be among her best volumes of poetry.[6] Her father had died in 1906, and this volume is tinged with the sadness and resignation she felt at this time. Six of the poems speak directly about her father and the love she had for him. George Russell, who knew her father, praised these poems particularly for the loving portrayal of Andrew Tynan.[7] In keeping with these touching poems recalling her father and her own relationship with him are a number of poems which speak of her longing for Ireland, including " 'Tis Hot Today in London" and "At Euston Station." Both themes combine in a touching lyric which exhibits Yeatsian overtones in its diction and subject matter, but which stands on its own as one of Tynan's better lyrics from this period. It is called "The Irish Pipes":

> I heard the piper playing,
> The piper old and blind,
> And knew its secret saying—
> The voice of the summer wind.
>
> I heard clear waters falling,
> Lapping from stone to stone;
> The wood-dove crying and calling,
> Ever alone, alone.
>
> I heard the bells of the heather
> Ring in the summer breeze,
> Soft stir of fur and feather
> And quiet hum of bees.
>
> The piper drew me yearning
> Into the dim grey lands,

Whence there is no returning
Although I wring my hands.

There to the piper's crooning
I saw my dead again,
All in a happy nooning
Of golden sun and rain.

You piper, kind and hoary,
Your pipes upon your knee,
If I should tell my story,
The things you piped for me,

The folk would leave their selling
And bid their buying go,
If I could be but telling
The things you let me know.

This poem is proof that, even after a lapse of a decade, Tynan
was still able to produce poetry of beauty and meaning when she
turned to the simplicity of Irish images and Irish structures.

The death of her father affected Tynan in many ways. It
caused her to reflect on her early life; it forced her to rethink
her attitudes toward Ireland as her home now that her father
was no longer there. This reexamination of her feelings is obvious
in both "The Dark Rose" and "At Euston Station." Equally
important with her reflection on her father's life and her
consideration of her Irish identity is a new theme which becomes
noticeable in Tynan's writings at this time: her consciousness of
the passing of time. While her father lived, regardless of her own
advancing age, she was still able to perceive herself as a
daughter; he was her last link with her glorious and exuberant
youth. Now with his death came the realization of her own
mortality, the inevitable passage of time, the inexorable consciousness of change. She had always been full of the love of life
and this loss, this change wrought in her life, deepened her love
of life, intensified her appreciation of it. Life and love and joy
were fleeting, and her poetry at this time takes on a new energy,
a new commitment to preserve what is fleeting in the face of
death and change. "The Last Time," a poem in this collection,
written to her husband, whom she perceives in a new light since
her father's death, signals this new direction in her thinking and
in her poetry:

This is the last time we shall sit and see
The dreaming hills so dear to you and me;
The last time that this mountain wind so cool
Shall lave us in its freshness beautiful.

The last time we shall go in the dim dusk,
Down the steep golf-links, sweet with honey and musk
Of the evening fragrance; and the last sad time
We'll hear across these fields the vesper chime.

We shall not hear again the wood-doves all
Crooning, when shades of night begin to fall,
Nor smell again yon pines that fill the night
And day with their spilt odours of delight.

We shall not sleep and wake so fresh, so gay,
Under our cottage eaves to the bright day,
Nor see across the lawn the exquisite trees
Flinging long shadows over the pale leas.

Our life is full of last times; yet we go
With a high heart of courage, since we know
We go together, we and our small brood,
Dear imps of mischief, quaint and wild and good.

With a high heart of courage we can face,
Hand fast in hand, all change of time and place,
The dark fogs and the winter and the streets,
We have our secret greenness, our retreats.

Yet in all last times there is hid a grief,
A canker in the flower and in the leaf,
Over them lies a shadow not their own,
From some most bitter day, my dear, my own.

When for the last time I shall walk with you—
Even old friends must part though dear and true—
We who were always glad, being side by side,
Shall reach that point at last where ways divide.

And for the sake of the last talk, last walk,
To-night the flower goes withering on its stalk,
There's desolation on the hills and sea
Because of the last time that's yet to be.

VIII   Lauds

In 1909 Tynan published *Lauds*, a slender book of poems dedicated to her American friend and fellow poet, Louise Imogen Guiney. This volume is a reworking of many of the themes in the earlier book and includes a number of religious poems previously published in her book of carols. A number of the poems speak of her dead father, such as "The Tryst," which describes a visit to his grave, and "The Return," which describes a visit to his old room. A few also refer to her friend Mary who had died in the same year, especially "The Newly Dead." Tynan had the unfortunate habit, as seen in this volume, of imitating her own best work. She occasionally negates the poetic power of strong poems by producing paler or weaker versions of the same poems. In this case, "Endings" is very similar in theme and imagery to "The Last Time" but lacks its strength and immediacy. Likewise "In The Country" is very similar to the earlier poem "To The Beloved." Tynan's greatest weakness in her poetry was her lack of restraint: she wrote too much within too narrow a range of subject matter. In constantly reworking her themes, and consistently making use of the same images and references she occasionally lost the freshness and uniqueness of her ideas and her language. This fault occurs more often in her nature and religious poetry, but it did occasionally, as in the poems mentioned above, occur in her deeply personal lyrics.

IX   New Poems

New Poems, the volume Tynan published in 1911, is a collection of poems which had been published in newspapers or magazines during the preceding two years. It offers little that is new in the way of subject matter or poetic structures. The book is significant, however, for the two poems which illustrate Tynan's changing conception of herself and her central role. "The Mother" and "Vocation" examine her sense of her own identity as a mother at this particular stage of her life.

X   Irish Poems

By comparison, *Irish Poems*, published in 1913, is a significant volume in Tynan's poetic corpus, containing forty-six poems on a broad range of subjects and attempting various poetic structures. However, the title of the book, *Irish Poems*, is slightly misleading. She does not attempt in this collection any revitalization of her earlier goals—to write on Irish subjects in an Irish manner. Rather, she calls these poems Irish because they were written in her own spirit of celebration and regret on her return from England to Ireland after so many years of living away.

Sadness, regret, and loss form the theme of many of these poems. As with her father's death, her return to Ireland inspires in Tynan a consciousness of lost time, of time beyond recapture. Her father, the focus of her life in Ireland, is dead. So, too, are many of her very dear friends, especially Father Russell. Tynan's poems express both regret and guilt that she had not been in Ireland to share with her friends and family those precious hours. And, too, her return to Ireland, like her father's death, signifies to her, emphasizes, in fact, that she is no longer young, no longer an intimate part of that social and literary life which had once, long ago, swirled around her, the young and famous Irish poet. She writes of this in her poem called "The Meeting":

> As I went through the ancient town,
> Long lost and found once more,
> Oh, who is this in a green gown
> I knew so well of yore?
>
> Veils of enchantment hid the place,
> Hung every street and square:
> I felt the sea-wind in my face
> And ruffling in my hair.
>
> Oh town I loved so well and lost,
> And find again with tears,
> Your streets hold many a darling ghost
> And all the vanished years!
>
> My heart went singing a low song,
> Glad to be home again.
> But who is this come blithe and young,
> Not feared of life but fain?
>
> Oh, who is this comes cold as stone
> To my quick cry and call?
> Of all the faces loved and flown
> I knew her best of all.

"Stay, you are . . ." Is she deaf and blind
Or hath she quite forgot?
What chill is in the sun, the wind,
Because she knows me not?

As I went down—my eyes were wet—
Eager and stepping fast
That was my own sweet youth I met
Who knew me not and passed.

Happy as Tynan had been in England, and much as she had come to love and appreciate its people and its way of life, she was overjoyed to return to Ireland. More than half of the poems in the volume speak of this joy: " 'Twas worth the years of exile just to recapture/The old delight, the wild bliss of coming back." Many of the poems are dedicated to her Irish friends and to those English friends who sped her on her way back to Ireland, who made the path easier for herself and her husband.

One poem, which exhibits her youthful command of the longer poetic line and lushness of natural description, is the poem entitled "Gorse" which she, significantly, dedicated to "W. B. Yeats who taught me":

Many a year I loved the gorse on an English common,
Miles on miles of the golden cups and the nutty wine,
Cloth of gold for the tramping folk, poor men and women;
Still my heart said in complaint: It is not mine.

Here's a golden wall each side the hill we're breasting;
Never sure was the English gorse as great as this!
Grapes of gold from a golden vine for the wild bees' questing:
A world of gold and a pearly cloud on a blue abyss.

There's a golden hill behind us now, gold on the azure,
The dearest hill like a little breast in gold above.
The lark springs from a golden bed, spilling his treasure,
Down on the buttercup fields of light and his hidden love.

Over the hill we bathe our feet in golden water,
A little stream the traveler fords, so clear and cold.
But is it May of the leafing—the High King's daughter
For all her green is under the wave of the flooding gold.

Over the hill—the yellow hill, the Spears are showing,
The Silver Spears are turned to gold o'er the valley's maze.
There's a small gold shower on the mountain now and the river flowing
Flows in and out like a ribbon of gold through the Milky Way.

The eager bees plunge to the thighs in a brimming chalice,
Their bags so full of the golden spoils they scarce can fly—
The mountain calls to the mountain now, over the valleys,
"Friend, we are Kings in the house of Kings, you and I."

Here with a heart fed of delight as a bee with honey
I sit like a miser counting the gold, nor shall repine,
For the cuckoo's roaming the golden street, blithesome and bonny—
My heart says to my heart: Have peace: this beauty's thine.

CHAPTER 5

The Later Poems

BY 1914 Tynan was installed in a large house near Castlebar, County Mayo, and her husband was working as a poorly paid but prestigious resident magistrate[1] whose duties required him to travel about the region, often staying for a number of days in each locality, holding petty sessions, and administrating local justice. A job which had once been the preserve of the second sons of wealthy families who could well afford the traveling and entertainment expenses involved, it was, in 1914, a demanding and tiring occupation with little monetary reward. The house which was provided as part of the remuneration did not belong to them, and, eventually, they were told to move yet again to another house, Brookhill, which Tynan came to love.

She was lonely in Mayo. Accustomed to the active social life of London and Dublin she noticed her isolation from the country people of her new region. With her children at school and her husband occupied with new responsibilities, she felt deprived of those activities and friendships that were so important to her. However, as always when she was presented with a challenge, Tynan rose to the occasion. She continued to write her novels and to maintain her contacts with her publishers and her distant friends.

I The War Poetry

The sounds of a world at war eventually penetrated even into the reaches of Country Mayo, and, distant though she was from that world of action, Tynan began to find herself deeply involved. In response to hearing of the tragic deaths of young English soldiers, some of whom she knew through their parents, Tynan began to write poems which expressed her own sense of sorrow and her compassion and empathy with those bereaved families. In *The Years of the Shadow* she wrote: "Quite early in the War letters began to come to me from the mourners. A poem of mine in the *Spectator,* Flower of Youth, had apparently caught and held many. Since it first appeared in the Autumn of 1914, it has brought many hundreds of letters. I believe I have written better poems of the War, or as good, but nothing I have written had approached its popularity. . . ."[2]

She wrote hundreds of war poems in the next four years, and these were published first in newspapers and periodicals and then published in four collections: *The Flower of Youth: Poems in War Time* (1915); *The Holy War* (1916); *Late Songs* (1917); and *Herb O'Grace: Poems in War Time* (1918). She also published *The Flower of Peace: A Collection of Devotional Poetry* in 1914, a selection from her previously published religious and inspirational verse grouped according to subject matter.

Two stanzas from Tynan's dedicatory poem which introduces her volume, *The Holy War,* describe her intentions in publishing her war poetry and the audience which she expected for these poems:

> These to the mourners of the war
> Saints of the great days, still and calm
> Who carry affliction like a star
> Who for your wounds have found a balm.
>
> For you, for you, unknown and dear,
> My bundle of woundwort's plucked again
> In this most glorious day and year
> That gives your man to die for men.

Throughout the collections of war poems run two parallel motifs: the heroism of the soldiers and the heroism of the families, especially the mothers and wives of these soldiers who died for the great cause. The first motif leads to the unquestioning assumption that the war was just, and that the boys who died all died bravely, heroically, and gladly for a glorious cause. All classes, all religions, all types, are made one in the great conflict. The body of the war poetry presents the war as a great challenge to be met, a proving ground of the spirit, where death and suffering have both a cathartic and levelling effect. Death, in the poems, is the great equalizer: it comes to all these soldiers equally, and in the fact of their death they achieve entry into that great aristocracy. They are heroes who all share in the honor, glory, and nobility most would never have achieved in ordinary life. In her poem, "The Children's War," this attitude is evident in a few representative lines:

> It is the Boy's War. Praise be given.
> To Percivale and Galahad
> Who have won earth and taken Heaven
> By violence! Weep not, but be glad.

The admonition in the last line occurs frequently in her poems of consolation. Acknowledging the great sorrow of loss, she offers as compensation to the bereaved the image of their own heroism. Advising them to be strong, to bear their suffering gladly, knowing they have sacrificed their flesh and blood to a larger cause, she praises their own courage and their own strength. Her message to the grieving was all the more powerful because her own sons were fighting in the war, perhaps side by side with the sons of the people who read her poetry. She, too, was a part of that great sisterhood who waited at home, anxious and worried. Fortunately, her sons survived the war, but, at the time of the writing and publishing of those poems, Tynan shared in the suffering and anxiety of those for whom she wrote. Naturally, then, in her poems she acknowledges this by stressing the shared nature of her message. In her poem, significantly titled "To The Others," she writes of this sharing:

> Your son and my son, clean as new swords,
> Your man and my man and now the Lord's!
> Your son and my son for the Great Crusade,
> With the banner of Christ over them—our knights, new-made.

As was natural for Tynan in time of distress and fear and powerlessness to alter circumstance, she, like many others, turned to the consolation of her religion. The poems are filled with the conventional, familiar, and comfortable Christian wisdom. The two greatest consolations that her religious sense perceives are, first, the transfiguration into heroes of those who die in a just cause; and second, the conviction that these dead men will find happiness and peace in heaven. This heaven of her imagination very much resembles the earth and those aspects of earthly life which she saw as happy and good. It was a theme which was to survive the period of the war poetry and which would be explored in her later lyrics. The heaven she describes is one certainly familiar to her readers, filled with warmth and light and totally accessible to the imagination. Never one for exploring the more theological aspects of her religion, she inclined to portray a heaven within everyone's reach, a heaven not limited by denominational differences.

No one can doubt the sincerity or the sentiments which lie behind the poems in these four volumes. However, sincerity does not necessarily make for great or, even, adequate poetry. Tynan's imagination was seldom engaged by large issues, great events, or historical movements. Her personality and her poetic gift were at their best when dealing with the immediate, the concrete, and the particular. Moreover, she was limited in these poems by her sole intention to comfort and to soothe the troubled spirits of her readers. Even if she had been so inclined toward the objective explorations of those emotions in poetry, the acknowledgment of a sense of bitterness, futility, and anger could not be permitted in poetry which aimed at a mass audience. Consequently, the themes are repetitive and limited; the imagery simplistic and recurrent; the religious thinking naive and childlike. The poetry seems to be mere verse making with simple rhymes and facile structures. The stories told in verse are very sad, and the overall tone of the books is sentimental.

These volumes are of little value in the consideration of Tynan's literary reputation today. They cannot be seen apart from their context, but they did serve a purpose outside the scope of art. The writing of these poems was important to Tynan personally, because isolated in County Mayo from the world she knew, a world in which she had always been actively and intensely involved, she found that the writing of the poetry and the maintaining of her massive correspondence with the readers of that poetry kept her active, and allowed her to make her own particular contribution. The popularity of the poems and the great and gratifying response she received point to the fact that she had indeed made a contribution to the society of her time. That even one person found consolation or a momentary appeasement of his or her grief through reading her poems was Tynan's only wish in the writing of them, and many people did find them a source of comfort. Since her motives were both personal and social rather than literary, these volumes can only be judged accordingly. They served the immediate purpose of reaching and, perhaps, helping the readers with whom she shared the anxiety of wife and mother. Read today, they do not stand among the great war poetry that contemporary poets produced, nor do they stand among her own best work. They stand as evidence of Tynan's own personal warmth, compassion, and love of people and her own continued trust in God. They reveal her own conservative acceptance of the structure of society and her continuing adherence to a spirit of resignation, perhaps inculcated in her thinking from her early religious training. In their way, the poems called for both spiritual courage and the setting up and veneration of new and unnamed heroes. Ironically, in this respect, they recall to mind those propagandistic poems which had filled her reading and experience in her youth and which, in finding her true poetic voice, she had abandoned. Her war poetry was limited by its motive, its audience, and its sentiment and now appears dated.

II *Poems About Death*

A substantial number of Tynan's poems deal with death and the intense longing of the survivor for one who has died. These poems fall into two categories: those poems written on the occasion of the death of someone she did not know personally, and this category includes her war poetry; the second includes poems written about the loss of people very close to her.

Even the casual reader will note the difference in style and tone which exists between the two categories. Those poems written during the war are indeed full of feeling and are obviously written by a woman deeply concerned. Written with the avowed intention of consoling those who had suffered the loss of son or husband, they are uniform in many respects, and consequently, rather impersonal. However, those poems written about her beloved friends are deeply personal and revealing of her attitude toward death itself.

One of Tynan's greatest gifts was her ability to develop and maintain strong and rewarding close friendships with many people. She was fortunate in their love and their friendship as she herself acknowledges many times in her books, but she was unfortunate in losing many of those closest to her in death. She outlived many of those early friends from her Dublin days and she felt their deaths keenly and deeply. To lose both her father and her dearest friend, Mary Gill, in the same year, 1906, was a heavy blow, and Tynan took a long time to come to terms with that blow. Almost always when most deeply moved, either by joy or sorrow, Tynan turned to poetry to express those deepest feelings. Consequently, a number of poems deal with Mary's death and with Tynan's great loneliness and longing for her father.

She writes in her reminiscences: "Of my father I desire to speak without a word of mourning. It is now seven years since he died and I no longer feel it is a profane thing to think of him or to speak of him as he was. His was so strong a personality, so living, that the note of mourning seems out of place. Somewhere he goes on living still, intensely human, simple, robust, great-hearted, kind."[3]

In her poetry, however, Tynan had felt free to speak of him. The intensity of her feelings found expression in the sanctioned poetic form. Her lyrics about him, being conceived of as art, were sacred rather than profane. She wrote many poems about him: a number are worthy of quotation for what they tell of the most central relationship in her emotional life, the relationship with the man whose influence and personality had shaped her thinking, her career, and her life. The sentiment behind the following poem needs little explication:

Everything that I made I used to bring to you.
Was it a song, why, then, 'twas a song to sing to you.
Was it a story, to you was I telling my story.
Ah, me dear, could you hear 'mid the bliss and the glory?

Did anyone praise me, to you I said it all over.
My laughter for you: how we laughed in the days past recover.
My tears and my trouble were for you: did anyone grieve me
I carried it straight to the love that was sure to relieve me.

O my dear, when aught happens, to you I am turning,
Forgetting how far you have travelled since then from my yearning.
There's nobody now to tell things to: your house is so lonely:
And still I'm forgetting and bringing my tale to you only.

The old days are over: how pleasant they were while they lasted!
The sands were pure gold that ran out ere we knew and were wasted.
And still I'm forgetting, ochone, that no longer you're near me,
And turn to you still with my tale, and there's no one to hear me.

Tynan felt the normal guilt of people who grieve for their
dead, and in the poem "Anniversary" this guilt had an immediate
cause. She had forgotten the anniversary of her father's death.
The day went by without her offering prayers for him, nor did
she think on his memory. In her dreams that night she dreamed
of him; he came to her as he had looked when she was young, and
they clung together; when they parted it was the "loneliest
parting under the moon." In this poem and in the former poem
Tynan does not mention the solace of religion which, in her less
personal poems, she offers to those bereaved. The emotion is one
of naked grief, a loss that cannot be compensated. True to her
own deep feelings, she avoids the easy solutions of many of her
war poems. Her particular sadness is inconsolable and at that she
lets it stand. Her longing to return to those happy early days
when she and he were young and together is sometimes painful
to observe. In the poem "For my Father" she again finds
happiness in a dream, no doubt both a waking and sleeping
dream, wherein she sees herself coming home to her father:

> Then I shall find you as in days long past,
> Sitting so quietly in the firelight glow;
> "Love," you will say to me, "you are come at last,"
> Your eyes be glad of me as long ago.
>
> All I have won since then will slip my hold,
> Dear love and children, the long years away:
> I shall come home to you, the girl of old,
> Glad to come home to you—oh, glad to stay!

Her poems capture the essential sadness and quiet despair of
loss. They deal openly and honestly with that moment when the
living recognize the irrevocableness of death. In the following
poem about her friend Mary's death, she makes use of the image
of the buds on the trees to indicate that immeasurable time that
exists between life and death:

When Mary Died

She only died last week and yet
Suns might have risen, suns have set
A thousand: May's here like a bride,
And it was May when Mary died.
. . . .
Last week! Why, this new grief we have
Is old as Time, old as the grave;
It was and will be: darkness spread
Over the world since Mary's dead.

Last week she died. The lilac-bough
Her eyes watched bud is blooming now;
The chestnut's lit her lamp since then;
And the lost cuckoo's come again.

A week ago! O endless space,
Since Mary heavenward turned her face!
And still the lilac's on the spray
That budded when she went away.

Tynan's poems about those people she knew and loved deeply
and for whom she grieves make use consistently of the images of
sleep and dreams. This constant linking of the two gives the
impression that the way in which she coped with her great losses
was to attempt to capture in her dreams the living personality of
those who had died. This is made most clear in her poem "The
Dreams," which also serves to remind the reader of how many
beloved friends and relatives Tynan had lost:

When I am sleeping I go in dreams
Far from the children and the man beside,
I meet with the dead and talk, nor strange it seems,
Since I've forgotten that they ever died.
. . . .
They come to me in my dreams, not cold and lone,
Oh, never sad ghosts they come to fret my sleep,
But just as I knew them in the days long gone.
When I wake from my dreams, I wake to weep.

That the solutions she offered in her war poetry were
inadequate for herself is borne out by those poems which she

wrote about her own personal losses. The reader immediately recognizes the intensity of her feelings and the fact that she does not picture her beloved dead in some heavenly home as consolation. These poems of anguish and longing portray Tynan finding relief only in dreams—both waking and sleeping—in which she sees and speaks with the dead. Many of these poems picture her returning to a time or a place long since past, returning to her youth, or to her girlhood home, and the sense of peace and satisfaction after years of yearning and loneliness is nearly tangible. They reveal her innermost feelings in a way her chatty conversational reminiscences never approach. Here one can read of a kind of loneliness that she never mentions in her prose and one for which her religion could not compensate. It is in these poems of death and loss and in those which deal with her dead children and her marital love that one comes closest to Tynan's inner self which the prose seldom reveals—a woman who had suffered and who did not find any easy solutions, but whose personal strengths and qualities helped her to cope when both life and religion failed her.

III   Late Songs

In *Late Songs* (1917) and *Herb O'Grace* (1918) Tynan included lyrics at the end of each collection which did not deal with the war and which fall into her long established categories of nature poems, inspirational poems, and poems which speak of her own personal feelings. *Late Songs* does not include any poems of true Irish significance. Two refer to Ireland and are in the mode of the poems of exile written when she was in England. One of the religious poems, entitled "Loneliness," has the most unusual theme of Christ's loneliness for his mother when He has ascended to heaven and she is still living on earth.

The overall tone of the poems in the latter part of the book is one of sadness, loneliness, and resignation. Three deal with the loss and death of her father and close friends; others deal with the deaths of children as in "The Newly Born." The tone of the volume is somber in keeping with events of her own life and, in a larger context, of Europe at war with itself. The awareness of the passage of time which entered Tynan's poetry after her father's death and her move back to Ireland now begins to predominate. Although not overtly stated, these poems when read together

point to Tynan's new consideration of her own life and
demonstrate an awareness of her age and mortality—of the
transiency of life. Her poems begin to talk, as they had not done
before, of her sense of the irrevocable as in "The Last Quarrel"
and of a new sense of the soul as in "The House of Life." In
keeping with her sense of the irreversible march of time is her
new habit of retrospection in her poetry.

Both "Sanctuaries" and "An Abiding City" mark new ways of
looking at the world. Although written in the language shared
with many of her inspirational poems these speak in a new way of
her relationship with her God. In the former she writes of that
world which God made and gave to her. In the latter she writes
of the city of God which lives within her. The two together speak
of the internalization of what had once been merely her love of
nature. Many of these poems, although they speak of God, cannot
be classed among her religious poems. They are personal lyrics
which begin to speak of her understanding and interpretation of
her own life and its relation to God.

In "The Recompense" and "The Tree" one can see Tynan
beginning to consider her own life in perspective. It is as though
after a life filled, more than most, with activity and people, she
has had at last the time, in Mayo, to approach the still center of
her life, her own being. The poems exhibit a sense of
retrospection and consideration of her past and a preparation for
the future, a reassessment of her values and her behavior, her
life and career, a clarifying of her own personal philosophy.

"The Recompense," although talking on one level of the story
of creation, speaks through that story of her particular under-
standing of marital love. The poem tells of the exile of Adam and
Eve from the garden, and how God pitied them and inspired
Adam to build a house to shelter himself and Eve, and how, too,
He taught them to make a fire for warmth and light:

> Yet there was something incomplete:
> They wept for their remembered blisses;
> Till God slipt something wondrous sweet
> Betwixt His anger and their kisses;
> The Woman shall make a Home: He said:
> With children, and the hearth-fire burning,
> And with her bosom for his bed
> My Adam praise Me night and morning.

Here, physical love, children, and the relationship between man and woman, husband and wife, are presented as adequate compensation for the loss of paradise. The poem reflects her own sense of completion which she found in marriage and children.

In "The Tree" this definition of her own identity is even more explicit. She uses one of her favorite images in this poem; the first line sets up the simile that is maintained throughout the lyric: "Think of her when she shall be dead/As of a kindly tree." The early stanzas ask the reader to think about the various facets of her early life: that she bore and cared for children; that she thought upon the Lord and praised Him in her work and deeds; that she was a source of comfort, peace, and hospitality for many people; that her children loved her. The last five stanzas state clearly how she wished to be remembered:

> Say that in Spring her boughs were green
> The joy ran in her blood,
> That Summer clad her like a Queen
> Under a velvet hood.

Using the conventional metaphor of the seasons to indicate the stages of her life, she continues. The use of the emphatic "but" which opens the final passage calls attention to her implicit desires—not so much to be remembered, but to live the latter part of her life with fortitude, enthusiasm, wisdom, and grace:

> But say that when her Autumn came
> Her best was yet to be:
> She clad herself in gold and flame
> Like to the Burning Tree.
>
> Say that she feared no Winter white
> In whose thin boughs did swing
> The moon, the stars, for a lantern bright
> To light the feet of Spring.
>
> Say that her head was never bowed
> Though trouble might befall;
> The bird in her heart sang low and loud
> And made amends for all.

> Say that in fine, her spring beside
> She was merry and gave grace,
> And some were sorry when she died
> Who lost a resting-place.

A poem in *Herb O'Grace*, the 1918 collection of her poetry, entitled "A Song of Going" likewise deals with the theme of aging. In this poem, the poet does not want to become old, in the sense that she will forget that it had ever been spring. The war poems apart, the remaining poems continue the themes of this middle period. Two are noteworthy as examples of both her fine eye for telling detail and the way in which she weds this to her true poetic talent, to the expression of her personal interpretation of God. In "Epiphany" she contrasts the very real and human infant Christ with the earthly kings who came to do him homage. The contrast is pointed by her setting the wealth of kings, "Myrrh, spikenard, such precious things" against "His mother's milk in a full tide." In a physical description unusual in conventional devotional verse, she highlights the very human aspect of the God made man:

> O'er Mother's breast His fingers go,
> Constraining that sweet stream to flow,
> So soft and small,
> To whom that milky world is all.

This sense for detail is also found in "The Image," a lovely poem with flowing rhythm and felicitous choice of rhyme. It is a mature poem which states clearly and simply Tynan's love of humanity and nature and her deep love of God. It is a mature vision and a surer statement of those early sentiments expressed in her devotional verse:

> When a wild grace I see
> A turn o' the neck, a curl, sweet hands, clear eyes,
> Gentleness, courtesy, dignity;
> In all these gifts Thee I surmise, surprise.
>
> All beauty and delight:
> Skin like a rose, a beauteous shape, and air
> Free and enchanting, give my weary sight
> Glimpses of Thee, Thou Beauty past compare.

Strength, courage also are Thine,
And joy of youth and wings that cleave the blue,
Low singing and soft voice: I divine
In these Thy beauty ancient yet ever new.

O, when my startled eye
Perceives this beauty league-long, sea and isle
And eagle-crested mountains wild and high,
I catch Thy Maker's thought—I see Thy smile.

Some mirror out of range
Flashes reflex of Heaven on this sweet earth,
Brooding for ever, beautiful, without change,
The bluebell sea, the thousand streams' soft mirth.

All beauty is of Thee:
Kindness and quietness, moon and stars and sun,
Gardens and woods, the bird in the new-fledged tree,
And sleep, O Kindest One!

Tynan's newfound sense of self and her new mature vision of life, of youth and age, of God, were to be challenged very much sooner than she had ever expected when she sat down in Mayo to write "The Tree." Tynan's husband died unexpectedly in his mid-fifties. His death was a great sorrow to her, deeper, perhaps, than any previous loss of father or of children, for she was unable to speak of it in her autobiographical writings. One recalls the poem written in the early days of her marriage wherein she refrains from speaking about her love for her husband, because silence and tears alone were adequate to its intensity. The silence about her loss is eloquent.

IV   Evensong

With the death of her husband, and without a pension and only a small income, Tynan was once more challenged to make her own living. The next few years saw many moves. Once the house in Mayo was closed and the furniture stored, Tynan was free to travel—to Dublin, to England, to visit friends and family. The title of her next volume of poetry, published in 1922 three years after her husband's death, is appropriately entitled *Evensong*, a title which reflects Tynan's own feelings about her life during this sad and difficult time and which indicates the overall tone of this collection of lyrics.

A number of poems refer directly to her feelings about her husband and her loss. In "The First Thrush" she recalls how she and her husband listened to the bird's song many years ago and how he must know, even though they are no longer together, what she feels and what she remembers. A poem in the same vein talks of their last days in Mayo "When he and I together, walked in wild weather." Although her memories provide some solace and comfort, they can at times, as in "Little Things," break her heart as she recalls a turn of his head or a look on his face. In "Last Year" she speaks of the time just twelve months before when her sons were home but her husband was gone from her in death. Although less than a year has passed, "so wide, so deep" was the chasm that parts them that the year could be fifty years. "In May" also speaks of her happy early days and makes use of the touching refrain: "Oh, love, remember yet." "The Morning Fields," although not written about her husband, reflects the same weariness and sense of sadness that fills those poems and which filled her life at the time. Unable to feel the same joy and peace in nature that she had previously experienced, these fields now depress her in their appearance.

The poem "Fiat," however, introduces a note of acceptance concurrent with those poems which speak of loss. In this she tells of her resignation to the will of God, as signified by the title, familiar to her from her religious training as the word spoken by Mary at the visitation of the angel announcing the birth of the child. "After Drought" which uses the image of cooling, satisfying rain falling after a long dry and sterile season continues the theme of resignation. "Thanksgiving," also a poem of resignation, expresses her gratitude for the quiet which follows the storm.

Her poems record her gradual acceptance of her husband's death and of her loss, helped by a spirit of resignation to the will of God. The poems continue to record her return to peace of spirit and her gratitude to God for those things which can console her: birds, a sunset, the reflection in nature of His love as in "The Light on the Water," a beautifully imaged short piece. In "The Message" she does indeed take the message, that God touches His own, to be hers; God has touched her husband in calling him in death; likewise He has touched her with a suffering, a cross to be borne willingly for His sake and for her soul's sake.

Her husband's death was a serious blow to Tynan in many ways. Not only had she lost his companionship and love but she had lost her home. A major theme in her poetry had been that concern for the home as a place of retreat, peace, love, and creativity. A major component of her self-image was her identity as wife and mother. With the death of her husband she lost one role. With the disbanding of the family home and the eventual marriage of her sons, she lost another. In the exigencies of their position Tynan and her daughter became friends and companions. At a time when Tynan could have looked forward, and did, to growing old with her husband, the substance of her dreams disappeared like smoke. Instead of being able to enjoy the relative comfort of a stable residence and financial security in company with her husband in the last decade of her life, instead of being able to devote her creativity to the mode of composition she had kept for art—her poetry—she was forced once again to face a new challenge, to travel, to live in numerous different houses and flats, to maintain her own life, to write her novels.

At times the burden is too heavy, and she longs, as in "The Secret," to return to Ireland: "Draw me home to rest" she asks of her spiritual and native home. Longing for a home of her own she prays to St. Joseph in the sweet poem "She Asks for a House."

Despite and, indeed, in response to the tragedy and consequent insecurities of her last years Tynan was able to achieve a spirit of faith and joy in life. Her poems in her later years speak of the triumph of faith and trust, of a spirit of optimism inherent in her youth but now tested and tried. The placid poems of her youth pale by comparison with those later poems which speak of a woman who has suffered and survived, a vision tempered but stronger, more mature, more joyful for its experiences and the personality which dealt with them.

Three major poems of her later career are collected in this volume, and in each of these are to be found the personal and poetic strengths of this final phase of Tynan's life and career. The first of these three is a prayer, written with the confidence and ease of one who has prayed many times throughout her life. The title "She Asks for a New Earth" states her desire, a desire which at first may surprise the reader unfamiliar with Tynan's life and spirit:

Lord when I find at last thy Paradise,
Be it not all too bright for human eyes,
Lest I go sick for home through the high mirth—
For Thy new Heaven, Lord, give me a new earth.

Give of thy mansion, Lord, a house so small
Where they can come to me who were my all;
Let them run home to me just as of yore,
Glad to sit down with me and go out no more.

Give me a garden, Lord, and a low hill,
A field and a babbling brook that is not still;
Give me an orchard, Lord, in leaf and bloom,
And my birds to sing to me in a quiet gloam.

There shall no canker be in leaf and bud,
But glory on hill and sea and the green-wood,
There, there shall none grow old but all be new
No rust nor moth shall fret nor thief break through.

Set thou a mist upon Thy glorious sun,
Lest we should faint for night and be undone;
Give us the high clean wind and the wild rain,
Lest that we faint with thirst and go in pain.

Let there be Winter there and the joy of Spring,
Summer and Autumn and the harvesting;
Give us all the things we loved on earth of old
Never to slip from out our fond arms' fold.

Give me a little house for my desire,
The man and the children to sit by my fire,
And friends crowding in to us, to our lit hearth—
For Thy new Heaven Lord, give me new earth!

In her new mood she is looking ahead to the end of her long life, and, in the conviction of her religious beliefs, contemplates that life after death. This poem, cast as a prayer, asks only of that heaven, that afterlife, that it resemble the happiest periods of her own life. Humbled and awed by what might lie ahead, she asks with the confidence and trust of a child that the heaven, the spiritual life which awaits her, will retain all that is familiar, comprehensible, and comfortable and secure. That her prayer is rooted in her own life is testimony to the joy and happiness she found in looking back over that life. Her desires are simple and nostalgic: she hopes for a small house, and her husband, children, and friends around her; a garden wherein she would find all the aspects of nature which she knew and loved; she even looks for that familiar wet and misty climate she knew in Ireland in all its seasons. Out of her long and full life that period of time she chooses to be her eternity encompasses those few short years when she had her youth, her security in her husband, and her fulfillment in her children and in her career.

The next poem, "The Purblind Praises the Lord," will recall the fact of Tynan's lifelong handicap, her very weak eyesight. Blind for almost two years in her childhood, her vision was impaired throughout her life. It is a fact she rarely mentions in her autobiographical writings. Although she wore glasses, she was so near-sighted as to be unable to recognize her friends in the street. Tynan never complained about her sight, and there are only a few poems which refer to the physical blindness in her entire corpus. However, in this late poem she does speak of it and finds even in that handicap something of positive value, something to be praised.

> They cannot know, the keen of sight,
> The lovely things I see.
> I praise the Lord both day and night
> That He remembers me.
>
> I see the tree in its new leaf,
> A Burning bush of green;
> Green beyond wonder and belief
> Its soft and silken sheen.
>
> I cannot see the birds in boughs,
> But an enchanted choir
> Sings all day long in a hid house
> Of emerald, flame, and fire.
>
> I cannot tell where hills leave off
> And where the clouds begin:
> Such mountains, Alp on Alp, above,
> No eye hath ever seen.
>
> Pink blossom on the apple-branch
> For me's a rosy bower—

The cherry tree an avalanche
Of snow-white flower on flower.

My distant cable's misted round
With gold and glittering air,
An angel with a glory crowned
Upon the heavenly stair.

I miss the common and the dull,
The small details of things,
And only keep the beautiful,
The stars, the flowers, the wings.

I see faces that are dear,
The others they may pass.
I thank my God I see not clear,
But dim, as in a glass.

Yea, though the world should slip from sight
And I no more should see,
I'll praise my God both day and night
That he remembers me.

This poem is characteristic in tone and theme of the later poetry of Tynan stemming from her new mature philosophy. The poem unintentionally reflects the way she looked at the world not just physically, but with the eyes of her soul. Her spiritual vision was such throughout her life that she saw reality through a particular prism. She well knew of suffering and pain; she knew about insecurity and death; she knew tragedy and loss and disappointment, and yet she struggled to see these in the light of God's will. It was her vision, a Christian vision, to see such good in all people, to find the good in one's self and in the circumstances of one's life. It is important to remember when reading these poems of Tynan's faith and optimism that she viewed the world clearly but chose to "only keep the beautiful." Through personal loneliness and real difficulties, she had attained to a vision of the world as a beautiful place that heaven should resemble.

Also included in this volume is the poem "Personalia" which George Russell chose to open his edition of her collected poems. This is a poem remarkable for its statements: a summary of

Tynan's long life and career and her retrospective interpretation of it. Full of serenity and a beautiful calm, it is simple and touching—a perfect example of her later poetic style:

> I was born under a kind star
> In a green world withouten any war;
> My eyes opened on quiet fields and hills,
> Orchards and gardens, cowslips, daffodils,
> Love for my rising-up and lying-down,
> Amid the beautiful pastures green and brown—
> The rose leaned through my window set ajar—
> I was born under a kind star.
>
> In a green land without hunger and drouth,
> God gave a gift of singing to my mouth,
> A little song and quiet that was heard
> Through the full choir of many a golden bird
> As a little brook in grasses running sweet,
> Full of refreshment for the noontide heat.
> Some came and drank of me from near and far—
> I was born under a kind star.
>
> I was fed full with bliss past my desert
> And when grief came, was comfort for my hurt.
> I had long nights of sleep that had no ear
> For the struck hours, the shrilling Chanticleer.
> My days were busy and glad from day to dark,
> My heart leaped high and merry with the lark.
> I shall die young though many my years are—
> For I was born under a kind star.

In the last stanza of this poem Tynan is grateful for the nights of untroubled sleep which she was fortunate to have. Many poems throughout her corpus speak of this need for undisturbed sleep. From early childhood she had been very much afraid of the dark and, whenever possible, had slept with a light in her room. The night had terrors of its own—memories, loneliness, and fear which only sleep could dissipate. Her poems about sleep and dreams show how she found surcease from sorrow in her life. Sleep relieved it, and dreams enabled her to see and speak again with all her beloved dead. Her volume of poems ends with "The Two Voices" which, coming so closely to "Personalia" which immediately precedes it, serves to highlight that the vision and

attainment of the previous poem was not lightly won, nor was her
sense of contentment and peace an entirely stable and unchang-
ing one. "The Two Voices" speaks not only of the fast
approaching night but of death and tribulation of spirit:

> The night darkens fast and the shadows darken;
> Clouds and the rain gather about mine house.
> Only the wood-dove moans—hearken, oh, hearken!
> The moan of the wood-dove in the rain-wet boughs.
>
> *Loneliness and the night! Night is not lonely;*
> *Star-crowned the night takes to a tender breast,*
> *Wrapping them in her veil these dark hours only,*
> *The weary, the bereaved, the dispossessed.*
>
> When will it lighten? Once the night was kindly
> Nor all her hours went by leaden and long.
> Now in mine house the hours go groping blindly
> After the shiver of dawn, the first bird's song.
>
> *Sleep now! Be still! The night with wings of splendour*
> *Hides heavy eyes from light that they may sleep,*
> *Soft and secure under her gaze so tender,*
> *Lest they should wake to weep, should wake to weep.*

This poem, which George Russell placed at the end of the
Collected Poems, indicates how, indeed, Tynan viewed herself in
the lonely reaches of the night, "weary, bereaved and dispossessed": weary of the long fight to live and work; bereft of
her husband, father, and friends; dispossessed of both her
physical and spiritual home. As in those poems in which she finds
no surcease from grief except in dreams, in "The Two Voices"
she finds no rest from the troubles surrounding her like clouds
and rain unless sleep closes her eyes against those things that
cause her to weep. The poem, too, is strongly suggestive of the
sleep of death, a theme which was to occur in her final volume of
poetry.

V Twilight Songs

Evensong was followed, in 1927, by Tynan's aptly titled
Twilight Songs, dedicated, significantly, to her large and faithful
readership: "To those for whom these were made." It is an

uneven volume as all of Tynan's collections of her poetry tended to be—from insignificant and weak poems to others which exhibit her true poetic power.

Her interest in truly Irish subjects and forms had long since faded. Unlike her old friend Yeats who, in his later poetry, found new strength in the ballad form and in his Irish identity, history, and experience, Tynan had abandoned the ballads, the narratives, the poems of Irish reference and meaning. The few poems which deal with Ireland in her last volume are merely nostalgic reminiscences of her own personal happiness there. By 1927, and after a long and varied life, the youthful vigor, faith, and ambition of those early days of the Irish literary revival must have seemed very far away indeed. She had attempted, on her return to Ireland, to reestablish contact with the literary milieu she once knew so well. She took a keen interest in the work of the younger generation of poets and hoped that it would be possible to establish a literary circle. Always a good listener and a willing reader, she was available to that younger generation, but, isolated in Mayo and out of the mainstream of poets liberated by Yeats's advice and example, this hope proved difficult of fulfillment. The old circle of which she had been once so much a part had changed beyond recognition. Moreover, Tynan seems to have failed to realize the significance of the Easter Rising of 1916 and the subsequent political events in Ireland. Anglicized by her many years of living in England, preoccupied with the events of World War I, isolated in Mayo, she had lost touch with the political ambitions, the passions, the hopes of her own people. Her political involvement and, perhaps, her understanding of politics died with Parnell. She lacked an historical vision: time and history did not interest her except in the ways events affected the individual. Apolitical in her middle age and loving both countries which she had called home, she expressed the hope that the two could live in peace and harmony.

The events of 1916, the subsequent civil war, and the development of the new Irish Republic she viewed as disturbing. She pitied both sides in the conflict and she condemned violence wherever she saw it, particularly, mindless violence and the destruction of what was beautiful and harmonious. Again, unlike her youthful companion Yeats, her mind and imagination never became engaged by the political events of her native land. She longed for the life as it was before in Ireland, those early days of her youth. Its best attributes of order, graciousness, generosity, and culture she saw as being disrupted. She mourned the loss of manners and customs which had supported the peaceful conduct of one's life in society. Thus, her poetic statements are filled with longing and nostalgia, for Ireland, for her father, for her youth. In these poems her eyes are now turned to the past or into the future where death and heaven await. The past has become more vivid than the present in her poetry. And the future contains those elements of the past for which she longs. In "The Voyage" she writes of her coming voyage, her embarkation into death, but she is not filled with fear because love awaits her there. In "The Waking" she speaks of waking into death and new life in heaven, a heaven which is described in the poem "There" as a place where there will never again be any more partings or farewells.

This is her longing—for heaven, for peace, for a recapturing of those youthful days of life, love, and happiness. Having attained a measure of wisdom, having achieved certain insights and having expressed these, sometimes powerfully, in those poems found in the previous volume, perhaps she should have chosen silence. The poems of her final volume offer little that is new and much that is repetitive, sentimental, and weak in subject and verse. Only "The Old Country," which opens the book, exhibits Tynan's resonance, her exploration of a new unrhymed structure, her poetic vision, and her ability:

As I go home at the end of day, the old road,
Through the enchanted country full of my dreams,
By the dim hills under the pellucid o'er-arching sky,
Home to the West, full of great clouds and the sunset,
Past the cattle that stand in rich grass to the knees,
It is not I who go home: it is not I.

Here is the turn we took, going home with my father,
The little feet of the pony trotting fast,
Home by the winding land full of music of water,
He and I, we were enough for each other;
Going home through the silver, the pearly twilight,
I content with my father, he with his daughter.

Magical country, full of memories and dreams,
My youth lies in the crevices of your hills;

Here in the silk of your grass by the edge of the meadows,
Every flower and leaf has its memories of you.
Home was home then and the people friendly,
And you and I going home in the lengthening shadows.

Now I go home no more, though the swift car glides,
Carries me fast through the dear, the heavenly country.
No one knows me, the cottages show strange faces,
They who were kindly, who bid me "God save you!" of yore,
They are gone, they are flown, and only the country's the same,
And you sleeping so quietly under the grass.

Tynan's decision to use free verse for this poem indicates that the strength of the emotion and the simplicity of the expression could not be contained or intensified by the use of her customary rhyming. The poem has a strength of structure and statement which makes the reader wish she had attempted more in this mode. As it is, few of the remaining poems in the volume reach this level. She continues in her usual modes the songs of spring and of nature, of exile from Ireland, of religious feeling, and of the events of the War. Some of the poems are biographical in content, as is "The Child" in which she writes of the grandchild who, in his existence, is able to give her back "Youth and my lost lover/And all the precious things were mine and his."

It is fitting that one of Tynan's last poems recalls to mind her father and the intense and important relationship which they shared. She had lived many lifetimes since his death, and yet in the end it is he whom she remembers: "He and I were enough for each other." In her memory he is forever associated with her beloved home at Whitehall, the hundreds of acres of beautiful farm and field, the happiness and peace of nature. His personality was the touchstone against which she judged other men. His relationship predisposed her to warmth toward other men, toward the fulfillment of marriage and family. She had inherited his vigor and joy in life and his fellowman. He launched her in life and he launched her in her career, full of strength, courage, ambition, faith in God and in humanity, and, most importantly, in herself.

In this last poem Tynan herself reveals how clearly and surely she saw herself, her life, her ability, her career; how fully she appreciated all that life had brought to her; how grateful she was for what had been given to her:

Thanksgiving

I thank God when I kneel to pray
That mine is still the middle way

Set in a safe and sweet estate
Between the little and the great

Not troubled with wealth's care nor yet
Too poor, where needs that cark and fret

Push out sweet leisure and green nooks
And give no chance for talk and books.

I take my middle way between
The mansion and the lodging mean.

My cottage at the country's edge
Hath sweetbriar growing in its hedge.

Honesty, heartsease, and sweet peas,
Herb-benet, Love-in-idleness.

Give me a tree, a well, a hive,
And I can save my soul alive.

Yet be as poor in spirit as
The Poverello's Lady was.

I covet not soft silk or lace
Nor any lovely lady's face;

Nor yet would go in hodden grey;
But lawns and wool be my array.

I still may ask a friend to dine
And set him meat and pour him wine;

Nor count the coins within my purse
To see that I am nothing worse.

I thank God that my middle place
Is set amid such pleasantness

And not too high and not too low
The safe, untroubled path I go.

CHAPTER 6

The Irish Voice

D URING Katharine Tynan's long career she was responsible for editing a number of collections of Irish prose and poetry, for which she also wrote the introductions. These works, together with her books of nonfiction which dealt with Ireland, provide insight not only into her critical judgments and literary acumen but also into her own perception of her Irish identity.

I   The Cabinet of Irish Literature

The first of the two major works which Tynan edited was entitled *The Cabinet of Irish Literature: Selections from the Works of the Chief Poets, Orators, and Prose Writers of Ireland.* The first edition of this work had been published twenty years earlier in London, but, because of the great upsurge of native Irish writing in the last decades of the nineteenth century, it was decided that a new edition was needed. In 1900 Tynan was commissioned to undertake a major revision of the first edition and at the same time to bring it up to date by the inclusion of works by Irish writers writing between 1880 and 1900. It was a massive undertaking, since the edition was published in four large volumes running into hundreds of pages of double columns of print. The edition was suitable for home or library, bound in extra gilt cloth with emblematic designs on gold or green with gilt-edged paper.

The circumstances under which she had to do the revision and extension were curious. Because of the publisher's stricture, owing to the way in which the volumes had been originally printed, Tynan had to excise the same number of lines of print to compensate for the number of lines which she added in updating the fourth volume. Thus the printer could maintain the same number of lines as in the original edition. This restriction made Tynan's work doubly difficult, limiting her choices, and causing her to be governed in the length of her selections by what she could eliminate. Her compliance with such restrictive revision is testimony to her tremendous capacity for organization and self-discipline. As she notes in *Middle Years:*

I had spent most of the winter on a heart-breaking job, undertaken gaily with no appreciation of the labour it would involve. I had to revise a Cyclopedia Cabinet of Irish Literature in four large volumes, to bring it up to date by adding a volume of new writers, then to compress the whole into four volumes. The stereos were to be preserved as far as possible—so that if I took out three lines on a page I had to put three lines in their place. I did it in three months. Anyone else would have taken three years or a lifetime. I have not really explained the difficulties. . . . I made a very good fourth volume in the result, but it did not please everyone. My publishers did not like my exlusion of some few writers I thought unsuited to the Irish households which would purchase the monumental work. Mr. George Moore was one of these.[1]

In her preface to the new edition she explains that, in order to give room to the newer writers, she omitted the earlier selections from orators, divines, and militarists which had lost some of their original relevance with the passage of time. She acknowledges that she is entirely responsible for the added material and, to the modern reader, volume 4 is of interest because in it she placed her own particular choices. The selection is wide and representative of the new Irish authors and poets writing in English from the 1880s to the turn of the century. Three authors are of particular interest to the modern reader. The first is W. B. Yeats, whose likeness, beardless and with glasses, Tynan chose as the frontispiece to volume 4. She writes in the biographical sketch of the author that Yeats is "the most remarkable Irish poet of our generation" and that his poetry possesses "exquisite qualities of imagination and realization." Her selections from his poetry show astute judgment; she presents the early "Mosada" as well as passages from "The Wanderings of Usheen." The remainder are representative of Yeats' lyrical sweetness and narrative power. The lyrics and ballads she chose deal with Irish subject matter: "The Stolen Child," "The Ballad of the Foxhunter," "The Man Who Dreamed of Faery Land," "The Host of the Air," "The Lake Isle of Innisfree," "The Pity of Love," "The Lamentation of the Old Pensioner," and "The Ballad of Father Gilligan."

Unfortunately, Tynan does not include any selections from her own poetry. Perhaps this was due to editorial policy, but it would have been of interest to see which poems she chose to represent her own work. She does, however, include a selection from her husband's romantic historical fiction and she includes a biographical note. It is unlikely he would have been included otherwise, since Hinkson's work was of a minor order.

Forced by the inclusive nature of *The Cabinet* and by her publishers to choose from the writings of George Moore, one of the most successful Irish novelists of the time, she ignored the realistic writing of his masterpieces, e.g., *Esther Waters*, in favor of innocuous passages with harmless subjects, inoffensive to Irish households. Moore's realism was interpreted at that time in Ireland to border on the unacceptable, since his work dealt with subjects such as illegitimacy.

In general, however, *The Cabinet* was a success. Few people could have afforded to own the individual works of the hundreds of major authors dating from Geofrey Keating (ca. 1550) to the twentieth century which are represented in *The Cabinet*. Her lengthy introduction traces in a clear, concise prose the outline of Irish literature, from its earliest roots in the ancient past, through the dispersal of the bardic poets in the seventeenth century. She deals adequately with Anglo-Irish writing and the writing of the Irish people in English. Her informative remarks show evidence of an understanding of the history of literature in her own country and an acquaintance with the work of numerous writers, especially the novelists of the nineteenth century. She explains, adequately enough for the general reader, the connection between the political life and literary life of Ireland, even remarking, as Yeats was often to do, that the lack of political activity following Parnell's death was in great measure responsible for the beginnings of the Irish literary revival. At the end of the long introduction she calls for an unnamed critic of genius to guide the Irish writers. Her call was significant, since her friend Yeats was to become the critic of genius for that generation.

The contents of the introduction illustrate Tynan's keen appreciation of Irish literature in English and in translation from the Irish, and her clear understanding of the influences on the development of modern Irish writing. It gives substance to Yeats' comments of her role in the movement.

Her introduction bears out Yeats' opinions regarding Tynan's role in the literary revival. In this work, as in a number of others, her goals are seen to be at one with those of her early career. Yeats writes: "When Lionel Johnson and Katharine Tynan, as she was then, and I myself began to reform Irish poetry we thought to keep unbroken the thread running up to Grattan. . . . We sought to make a more subtle rhythm, a more organic form than that of the older Irish poets who write in English, but always to remember certain ardent ideas and high attitudes of mind which were to our imagination the nation itself, so far as a nation can be summarised in the intellect."[2]

II   The Wild Harp

Although Tynan's goals altered with time, age, and circumstance, she retained her interest in the work of the Irish writers, including her contemporaries and those younger poets who followed in the next generation. She maintained an attitude toward those younger poets such as Padraic Colum and James Stephens which she had earlier maintained toward her contemporaries. In 1913 she published *The Wild Harp: A Selection from Irish Lyrical Poetry*, aimed at an English readership. As she states in the introduction to this work, the volume deals exclusively with Irish lyric poetry in English written in the nineteenth and early twentieth centuries. The volume excludes humorous, reflective, and propagandistic (political) poetry; lengthy poems; poems showing their derivation from English influences; and poems already well known to English audiences. The principles of selection allowed her to choose from the older lyric poets, Mangan and Ferguson, through the verse of the new young poets including Padraic Colum, W. B. Yeats, and James Joyce. Many of her comments reflect her own attitude toward her own lyrical poetry and illustrate her perception of the lyric form. She notes that many of the lyrics are simple, wild, and brief because they are expressions of emotion, an emotion "too sharply felt not to be expressed simply." The selections represent her own discoveries, her own delights, particularly among the new poets. In a simple explanation for her English readers, her remarks recall the lengthier explanations in *The Cabinet*. She briefly recounts that in her youth the young writers were fed on the rhetoric of the political poetry of the *Nation* poets and the Fenians. She acknowledges again Yeats' liberating influence and his encouragement of the poets of his own generation to write on Irish subjects for the Irish people. Tynan criticizes Yeats' turning away from poetry to his work in drama and the Abbey Theatre, and, without the gift of foresight she viewed this as a permanent change in his creative life.

Her selection of poetry for this volume is remarkable for its range and perception. She is to be credited for her inclusion of three of James Joyce's lyrics among the ninety-three poems in the book: "Strings in the Earth and Air," "At That Hour," and "I Hear An Army." The young poets of his generation are well represented and, although she was guided in this by her friend Russell, the final choice was her own. The list of poets stands as evidence of the perception of her choice, because many indeed have stood the test of time and literary criticism. The Joyce poems are perhaps of greatest interest to the modern reader and are proof of the modernity of her poetic thinking. In a letter to Joyce in 1914 she thanks him with all her heart for enriching her book wonderfully, and she remarks that his verses are aptly titled, and are indeed the strings of a wonderful music, intangibly exquisite.[3] It is a letter written with great sincerity and in a tone of encouragement to the younger poet. Sensitive as always to the special needs of poets and retaining her genuine allegiance to Irish poets and writers, these two edited selections stand as testimony to Tynan's role in the formation of an Irish national literature and her importance as forerunner of the Irish poets of the twentieth century, particularly those who lived abroad.

As can be seen from these two works, although Tynan lived in England for nearly twenty years, she never gave up her allegiance to Ireland. It has been part of the aim of this study to consider Tynan as an Irish writer, one who can be defined as writing from her own experience as a native of Ireland, for an Irish audience, about Irish matters.

Tynan and her contemporaries in Ireland sought both an Irish and an English audience because they sought the English market. A writing career was not a profitable occupation in the Ireland of Tynan's time. With a small and generally impoverished population, Ireland could not support the young writers it produced. Thus, the question sometimes raised concerning Tynan's publishing in England, and often with an eye to the American market, can be answered in terms of money—the need for which compelled her to publish and profit.

Consequently, unlike Yeats and Hyde who tried to preserve the
life and art of the Irish people for its intrinsic interest, Tynan
followed the alternate tradition which attempted to explain the
native Irish to the English. Tynan's nonfiction particularly falls
into this category of writing.

III   *Tynan's Nonfiction about Ireland*

In 1914 Tynan wrote a book about Ireland for the series,
current at the time, entitled *Peeps at Many Lands,* and aimed at
the older child. It combines the geography, history, and
sociology of Ireland, and presents the information in a readable,
casual manner which would appeal to young readers. The book,
in this case, was aimed at an English audience.

Tynan was in a unique position. As an Irishwoman living in
England she knew both countries well. As a widely published and
popular author with many publications to her name, she was in a
secure position with publisher and audience alike. It is interesting to consider what she made of this opportunity to present
her native land to those children of England whose understanding of their troublesome neighbor might well be influenced by
what she wrote.

On the first page, after addressing her young reader, she
begins by pointing out the differences that the English visitor
will notice as he arrives in Ireland. The book is presented in the
format of a tour around the country and the journey starts off in
Dublin. She accounts for the differences she mentions by stating
that these are a consequence of the differences between the
races—Celtic and Saxon. This distinction, made on the first page
of the book, is essential to the rest of the book and to much of her
writing in general. She saw the people of her own country as
being a separate group from the English, who had, at an earlier
time, conquered them and imposed their language upon the
native Irish.

The sections of the book relevant to our discussion of her
understanding and presentation of her own country are those
which deal with the character of the people, her descriptions
and estimation of their traits and characteristics. To make her
points clear to her young readers she often compares and
contrasts the English and the Irish, and is favorable, sometimes to
the one, and at times to the other. For example, she writes:

The Englishman is simple, the Irish complex. The Anglo-Irish, who stand to most English people for the Irish, have had grafted on them the complexity of the Irish without their pliability. . . . They will tell you in Ireland that you have to go some forty or fifty miles from Dublin before you get into Irish Ireland. There are a good many Irish in Anglo-Ireland usually in the humbler walks of life, whence you shall find in Dublin servants, car-drivers, policemen, newspaper-boys, and so on, the raciness, the vivacity, the charm which in Irish Ireland is a perpetual delight.[4]

She finds from her own experience that these "Irish" are not only delightful but also virtuous and witty. She finds that beggars have a sardonic wit; the children of beggars are innocent and amusing. Of the appalling slums in Dublin at the turn of the century she tells the reader that the people of the slums are noisy and cheerful "no matter how poor they may be." This cheerful aspect of the poor pleased her. Not so the village poor scattered throughout the poverty-stricken countryside: ". . . There are in the Irish country, villages of an incredible poverty. The Irish village mars a landscape, whereas, so often in England one enhances its beauty."[5]

Throughout the text of this short book are scattered passages which state directly Tynan's opinions on the character of the Irish people. These opinions are offered as statements of fact, often given without illustrative examples or reasons explaining the development of the various facets of the Irish national character.

For example, she writes that the Irish are generous and that this trait is found in all classes. She claims the Irish are full of sentiment yet marry for money. Arranged marriages were common in the rural districts of Ireland and this, too, puzzles her. She observes that the Irish love the home but that they are not domestic, and wonders if this is, perhaps, because "the art of making the home pleasant is not an Irish art." She does not seek reasons for any of these social patterns or behavioral traits which she observes. Neglecting the remote and the immediate past of the Irish people, she takes them out of their own context and presents them without explanation. This shallow treatment of one of the oldest and most complex cultures in Western Europe becomes obvious in the following passage: "They are very religious, and accept the invisible world with a thoroughness and simplicity of belief which they would say themselves is their most precious inheritance. The Celt is no materialist. He does not love success or riches; most of those whom he holds in most esteem have been neither rich or successful."[6]

Her use of the word "Celt," in this passage and others, distinguishes for the reader between the people of direct Irish descent and those Anglo-Irish—products of the last three centuries of the English presence in Ireland. She does not elaborate on this distinction between Celt and non-Celt. She does not inform the reader that the native Irish had been deprived of education, land, the means of livelihood, by which they could have advanced themselves socially and financially. Nor does she explain that their religion—Catholicism—was, in some measure, a compensation for the lives of hardship and poverty they had to endure. She states as facts, as racial characteristics, features of the Irish people which had developed from the circumstances in which they had lived for generations.

In other places, she makes observations of a more casual and humorous nature. Thrift and punctuality are vices rather than virtues in the Irish. She admires the broad humor and the subtle quick minds of the people. She compliments them for their generosity, their hospitality, and their kindness to friend and stranger alike.

In two lengthy passages she summarizes for her English readers two aspects of the Irish personality, and in these offers her analyses of that personality:

The Irish are notoriously brave, yet they have a fear of public opinion unknown to an Englishman. Underneath their charmingly gay and open manner there is a self-consciousness, a self-mistrust. For all their keen sense of humor, they cannot bear laughter directed at themselves. They dread to be made absurd more than anything else in this world. They are responsive and sympathetic, yet too witty not to be somewhat malicious; and they are warm and generous, yet not always so reliably kind as a duller, slower people. They are irritable, so they are less tolerant of children and animals although they make excellent nurses. . . . They have no tolerance at all for slowness or stupidity, very little for ugliness or want of charm. They adore beauty. . . .[7]

With the rise of nineteenth-century European nationalism there developed in England, as elsewhere, a keen interest in the concept of race. The English had become intrigued with the late romantic idea of the Celt. Writers, thinkers, populists, gave currency to the idea of the Celt as melancholy, aloof, dark, mysterious. He was seen as sad and gay by turns, in touch, somehow, with the world of the fairy and the supernatural. The soft alluring beauty of the Irish countryside, punctuated by the tremendous bleakness and loneliness of the coast and the western counties, the quickly changing weather, the bogs, the mists, all lent themselves to the English picture of the Celt. In keeping with the preconceived idea held by her audience, Tynan describes the Celt in what would be comfortably familiar terms: "Did I say the Celt was gay and melancholy? He is exquisitely gay and most profoundly melancholy. He is in touch with the other world, yet desperately afraid of it, or of the passage to it, being a creature of fine nerves and apprehension. . . ."[8]

Three years after that book was written, the Irish would attempt the abortive Easter Rising which would lead, in time, to their political separation from England and to the establishment of the Irish Republic. The comfortably romantic, English notion of the land of mist and bog, of melancholy, lonely, mystical people would finally be dispersed by violence and bloodshed. But until that time the English picture of the Irish, despite the work of major writers, was formed and continued to be reinforced by writers such as Katharine Tynan.

That Tynan's presentation of Ireland to her young English readers was governed by the awareness of her large English audience can be seen in two final examples. The first is her treatment of the great famine of the mid-nineteenth century. The failure of the potato crop on which the Irish were almost solely dependent for their food, and the consequent famine, led to the deaths of millions of Irish people, by starvation and disease, and to the emigration of millions more to America, Canada, and any other country to which they could gain access. She notes in other writings that in her childhood she knew elderly people, survivors of that desperate period in Irish history. The sufferings of the Irish people had been horrible. The actions of the English government during this tragic period came in for much criticism at the time and subsequently.

Of this catastrophic event in Irish history, an event which was to have immeasurable consequences for the Irish people, Tynan writes merely that "In the early days of the nineteenth century grass grew in the streets of Dublin. Famine and pestilence followed each other in monotonous succession."[9]

Her euphemism for the famine, that grass grew in the streets of Dublin, occurs both here and in other works such as her *Book of Irish History* (1918). In keeping with her presentation of the Irish to the English, a presentation that neglects, if it does not omit, major historical factors in the life of the country, are the illustrations which accompany the text of *Peeps at Many Lands: Ireland*. On the cover of the book, which is olive green, is a picture of two strong, healthy girls: one is bare-foot, digging potatoes with a spade; the other is placing the potatoes in a woven basket. It is an outsider's picture of Ireland. It is not a picture the majority of Irish people would have chosen to epitomize their country for the English reader in 1914. Most of the illustrations are of pleasant, pastoral scenes and views that are, in tone and style, in keeping with the tenor of the book.

IV *Additional Evidence of Tynan's Thought*

In passages scattered throughout her autobiographical writings, Tynan discusses many of the same issues and events covered in this children's book. These are of interest because they are written for an adult audience in England and in Ireland.

As mentioned, she made a vague distinction between the Celt and the Irish in her thinking about Ireland. The Irish Celt, she claimed, dislikes and distrusts good works.[10] In another place she notes that the Irish Celt, like all imaginative people, has a feeling for rank and title and the pageantry of life.[11] She also comments that "The Irish . . . have need for a King."[12] The terms are vague and often interchangeable, since she, herself, had no real fixed definition of Celt or Irish.

She does tend to describe herself as a Celt, and, in one example, says "I had the self-consciousness and suspicion of the Celt in contradistinction to the Anglo-Saxon effusiveness and confidence in its kind."[13] Tynan does not seek historical explanation for these differences and is content to ascribe them to the concept of "blood." Owing to "blood" she feels at home with the Northern Scots—whom she finds to be very much like the Irish, humorous, imaginative, and shrewd.[14]

She often remarks on the Irish sense of humor and doubts at times whether the English middle class possessed any sense of humor at all. By contrast, she finds the English more emotional:

Once I lectured on Irish poetry to a Women's Literary Society in Tunbridge Wells and found that the poetry made an extraordinary impression. Some of my audience wept to the pathetic poems, which proves my theory that the English are a more emotional people than the Irish. I have repeated the same poems to dry-eyed Irish audiences, although the poetry may appeal to other emotions.[15]

This passage contans some unintentional humor of its own. Apparently Tynan needed only slight proof indeed to prove her theory. Her use of the word "emotional" is vague. Perhaps by this she intended to say "sentimental," because numerous passages in her autobiographical writings describe the emotional nature of the Irish.

Many of her ideas on the subject of the Irish people appear to have been inherited from those around her. She uses worn-out phrases to describe stereotypes. One passage will suffice to illustrate this habit:

But after all, we quicken to the Lost Cause in an exaltation the placid and prosperous might well envy us. We have the necessity to fight for our cause and it must be a losing or lost cause to inspire our utmost devotion. Sorrow wears for us a more alluring face than joy, and our Queen must be in chains to win the heart out of our breast.[16]

Tynan writes with passion about this supposed characteristic of the Irish but does not support it with example or fact. She generalizes Ireland's history and then, in turn, romanticizes its people, using cliché to flesh out stereotype.

Tynan's indulgence in stereotype is reflected in her own use of the word "type." The sentences which follow are a mere twenty pages apart in her book, *Memories*. They illustrate first, that her writing style was repetitive and formulaic; and second, that the ideas expressed were likewise formulaic.

The first illustrative sentence describes the Right Honourable Mr. Justice Gibson: "He was the type of the old Irish gentleman which has passed or is passing. Ireland used to be full of them, young and old. I dare say that the type was gayer, more debonair, a little wilder, more charming at its best, than the gentlemen of other countries."[17]

The second sentence describes Percy French, the Irish composer: "He was a type of the Irish gentleman; and there is no finer type, gay and with laughter, easy and without conventions, somewhat wild and always a sport; these things differentiate the type from the gentleman of other countries; and to it Percy French belonged."[18]

This picture of the country gentleman, of which she very much approved, was formed in her youth by the force and appeal of her father's personality. In one revealing passage she writes of that personality: "Any picture of him that did not present his broad and humane humour must be incomplete. . . . I doubt that he was ever popular with his own class. With the people and with a higher social class he was very much admired and loved. The peasants, servants, tramping people, beggars and the like, had an appreciation of him as he had of them. They never resented it when he was violent with them."[19]

Of her own servants she tells that her domestics often left of their own will because of her "driving them with too slack a rein,"[20] and that the chief cause of servant trouble was the inability of the mistress to rule. She characterizes her servants in her nonfiction as she does in her novels: either they are real ladies in disguise or gifted with a mysterious ability, or they were useless; she seldom characterizes them as individuals but as belonging to groups with stereotypical characteristics.

In those passages in which she deals with the Anglo-Irish she talks of those peasants and domestics who served the Anglo-Irish class. She points out this class idealized the peasants, neglecting to see how she herself idealized them and then contributed to their idealization in her writings:

What the Irish Catholics called "The black Protestantism" of the Irish-Anglo gentry was in abeyance when it came to their Irish Catholic servants. There was often the most tender attachment between them. The children of the Normans had been fostered by Irish mothers and not all the Poynings Acts ever imagined could sever that soft and milky bond. The relationship persisted with the "new" gentry who were the result of various plantations; so that people to whom the name of priest was anathema and the Chapel—they would not concede it the name of Church—was the House of Rimmon, yet gave their children to Irish nurses, and in their most impressionable years, smiled upon the warm ties of affection between them and the people in the kitchen, the gate-lodge and the cabins outside.[21]

Consequently, because of her own class prejudices, she tended to identify with the native Irish gentry of which she saw her father as the epitome and, also, with the Anglo-Irish upper class. Her attitude toward the peasant was that attributed to the class with which she identified. However, she was neither a member of the upper class in Irish society nor a member of the people of rural Ireland. Belonging to neither, and becoming acquainted with them as an observer, she formed a superficial understanding of these classes which is reflected in both her nonfiction and her novels.

CHAPTER 7

The Early Fiction

DURING the early years of the last decade of the nineteenth century a demand had sprung up in English publications for "stories illustrative of peasant life and feeling in their simpler aspects and variations,"[1] and consequently, Tynan found herself writing sketches of Irish country life for the various English journals.

She writes in *Middle Years* that at this time (1891-1892):

I used to find material for sketches in the life about me. This I found to be a dangerous practice. My sketches were all idyllic and, of course, there was a very slight substratum of truth in their happenings. As for the people, they were so idealised from the original suggestion that if any thought he or she had been portrayed, he or she should have been immensely flattered. But, while that might apply to English people it did not to the Irish, who are very resentful of exploitation.[2]

This resentment of the Irish toward being exploited, particularly in literature, had a long history. The Irish people had been an object of fun in segments of the English press throughout the nineteenth century, and were often represented as buffoons, dunces, or illiterates. These publications had an underlying political aim of ridiculing a country toward which the English government owed an historic responsibility. In time, the harshness of these portrayals was modified. The Irish were then portrayed as a simplistic people of little or no culture, superstitious, naive, believing in the little people, the leprechaun. This treatment was equally damaging. The late nineteenth-century figure of the "stage Irishman" even today influences those who are unfamiliar with the Irish people and has contributed to the particular Irish stereotype of hard-drinking, hot-tempered, smooth-talking sentimentalists.

The exploitation of the Irish people by means of the written word was a particularly effective weapon because the Irish have traditionally held a deep respect for literature and the power of the word. This respect is consistent with the original Celtic culture. The oral poets of Celtic times, because their poetry embodied the history of the people, of the ruling tribes and families, were protected and nurtured under a sophisticated system of patronage. Furthermore, because of unique elements in the original Gaelic culture where the concept of saving face was central to the maintenance of authentic authority and kingship, the poet held a central and powerful position. Satire was a finely developed element in the poet's highly skilled repertoire. A cutting, caustic, subtle, and sophisticated satire directed at a king or member of the ruling family could cause the ruler to lose favor before his people because of the basis of truth which the satire would contain. Although the poets were generally supported by a particular family, the poet was essentially an independent individual who could also direct his satire against the family who protected him. Because of the powers accorded the poet he was treated for generations with the awe and respect also accorded the members of the priestly class, whether pagan or Christian. With the dispersion of the major ruling Irish families, called the Flight of the Earls in Irish history and legend, the system of patronage which supported the literary class, the oral poets, declined and their primary function was lost in the destruction of the culture in which they played an integral part. Although, from the seventeenth century, the established societal role of the poet declined, the power, the genius, and the effectiveness of satire was retained in the Irish people. Likewise, they remained sensitive not so much to satire which they could appreciate, but to ridicule in all its forms.

Tynan did not write her sketches with the intention of either ridicule or satire. She wrote for a new market keen to read about the peasant and rural way of life. Urban dwellers in London and elsewhere wished to read of a gentle, pastoral people, with a bit of humor thrown in to entertain them. These sketches of Tynan's, written about her fellow Irish, were written to entertain, and throughout her career she was periodically amazed at people's adverse reaction to being made use of as subject matter for these little sketches.

A number of these sketches were published together in her first book of fiction, entitled *A Cluster of Nuts: Being Sketches*

Among My Own People. It was published in 1894 under both her maiden and married names and dedicated to Mary Gill. Quoted on the title page is the rather puzzling line: "Kindly Irish of the Irish, Neither Saxon nor Italian." The volume opens with a poem, Irish in reference, entitled in Irish "Mo Craoibhin Cno," meaning my cluster of nuts. Addressed to the reader, it says, "Russet and small, but still within the brownness/May hide some sweetness— pray you find it so."

The first story, entitled "A Village Genius," concerns a shoemaker, well known to Tynan from the village near her home. She wrote often of this shoemaker in both her fiction and nonfiction. A poorly educated young man, he wrote stories which she read and criticized for him. It is apparent in her references to him that she used him as a figure of romance and transformed him into a symbol of that Ireland which the Irish literary movement under Yeats was trying to regenerate. Yeats, in an effort to revitalize the culture and thus the literature of his people, had early produced a number of volumes of myths, fairy tales, legends, and stories revolving around the people of the rural areas of Ireland. Tynan had her shoemaker manqué after the manner of Yeats, ascribing to the poor shoemaker the feelings of the literary person. In the last paragraph Tynan's grand style takes over: "The Round Tower knows the secrets of the upper air, but the quiet dead lie at rest in the earth amid the growing things, and in the hope of a glorious immortality. There the village genius has learned masterfully intimacy with familiar things, and the last great simplicity of death."[3]

Many of the incidents recounted in these sketches are told in more detail in Tynan's autobiographical works, illustrating how closely she used her own experience. A number of the stories deal with the emigrants leaving for America and leaving poor elderly parents behind them to mourn. Some of the stories deal with the Irish people whom Tynan observed when she was first living in England. Others deal with the domestic tragedies of people not as idealized as Tynan's comments lead one to expect. In "A Martyr Indeed" she tells the sad tale of a man whose mother and sister were alcoholics and who, as a result, never married the girl he loved. A single comment in this story illustrates Tynan's understanding of the simple people of whom she wrote: "For the Irish peasant though you can be extremely friendly with him or her, knows just where an equal familiarity begins, and is apt much to despise folk who cannot keep their places."[4]

The stories are written with that casual ease and conversational style which were to enable Tynan to write so many of these sketches over the years. The book lacks an overall sense of purpose. The stories are not chosen to provide contrast nor are they grouped according to an external plan. They are merely published together as a collection. They are obviously directed to an English audience because of the way in which she explains items and customs that would be familiar enough to the Irish reader. Throughout, the tone of the prose is that of an objective observer.

Although Tynan's sketches were written and presented as fiction, both the tone and the subject matter of the works place them in an indeterminate genre between nonfiction and fiction. However, her sketches did lay the groundwork for her work in the genre of the novel. The writing of the sketches taught her to observe character in action, to note personal characteristics of dress, speech, and behavior. She learned to detect in the actions and the life stories of those around her the seeds for the numerous plots which sustained her many novels. The writing of the sketches finally encouraged her, in 1892, to try her talent in the larger fictional form—the novel.

The literary tradition of the Irish novel against which backdrop Tynan began to write was strong but narrow. The early nineteenth century had produced certain literary masterpieces: the works of Maria Edgeworth were available to Tynan in her girlhood, as were the works of Samuel Lover and Charles Lever. Thomas Flanagan notes in his work on the subject,[5] that the ordinary reader of these novels accepted as fact that the characters in the novels stood in particular relation to one another: the gentleman, the man of class standing, property, or power was a Protestant: his retainers, members of the lower class, were Catholic. This traditional literary treatment reflected in general the reality of life in Ireland. The British and the Anglo-Irish readers of the novels were content to see that reflection of the social order in the literature. The idea of an Irish Catholic gentleman was alien to such readers although not quite so rare in reality as they were scarce in literature.

The landed Irish Catholic gentry who had survived the vicissitudes of the history of their native land were a conservative lot. They wished to live in harmony and prosperity, maintaining and improving what they already had, and they inclined to maintain the status quo for their own benefit. Their power was negligible in comparison with the real, social, and financial power of the Protestant ascendancy, and they did not hope to challenge it.

Flanagan also points out further elements in the tradition of the Irish novel which are likewise found in Tynan's novels set in Ireland. One of these is the presence of the ruin. In Tynan's novels the ruins take the form of the decaying great house and lands, neglected graveyards, ruined towers, and deserted monasteries, and do not point to the ancient order of Celtic life but to the then recent decline of the native aristocracy and landed gentry stemming from political and religious differences. The second element is the figure of the peasant in Irish writing. Like the stage Irishman, the fictional peasant is presented as an amusing figure—poor, dirty, but generally possessing native wit and cunning. Tynan's peasant figures for the most part follow in the tradition of Maria Edgeworth's vividly drawn characters, and she generally causes them to speak in dialect to indicate their different speech and class. The third element is the adherence of the native population to their Catholic religion viewed as a repository of ritual, symbol, society, and art—all unavailable to them in their ordinary circumstances of life. The superstitious and ritual aspect of Catholicism in Ireland figures more significantly in Tynan's novels than the purely religious aspects. The only significant religious aspect she includes is the appeal of the convent life for the poor but refined daughters in her novels.

I The Way of a Maid

In 1893 Tynan happily arranged her first novel, *The Way of a Maid*, with her publisher. This was also the idyllic, first year of her marriage to Henry Hinkson, whom she married in London in May. She writes that she came "home very happy with a cheque in my pocket. I shall not say how little or big it was. It was at all events big enough for happiness and a bottle of champagne. In those reprehensible early days we often treated ourselves and each other to champagne. . . ."[6]

In her volume of memoirs, *Middle Years,* she writes at length about this significant period of her creative life:

My literary doings were many. My industry, as set forth in the pages of my closely written little diary, amazes me. My voluminous reviews for the Irish Daily Independent, my couple of American Literary Letters— the Pall Mall Gazette, the Westminster, the National Observer, the Speaker, the Sketch, the Graphic, the Illustrated London News, many magazines: I think at one time or another I must have written for nearly every paper and magazine in London. . . .

Meanwhile my first novel was on the stocks. It was undertaken at the suggestion of Messrs: Lawrence and Bullen, the most unconventional and delightful of publishers. Lawrence and Bullen had published my "Cluster of Nuts," a volume of short Irish sketches, contributed to the National Observer, the Speaker, the Pall Mall, and elsewhere. Now they suggested a novel.[7]

The Way of a Maid was published in London in 1895 under Tynan's maiden name with her marriage name on the title page. She continued this procedure throughout her career, publishing always under her maiden name, the name under which she had established her reputation.

The action of her first novel is set significantly in Ireland, in a typical Irish country town called Coolevara. Tynan describes its river, hills, and airy plateau with her usual attention to details of nature and the countryside. The plot deals with two local families. The Hurley family are Catholics, simple people but descended from good old stock. The son, Jim, is engaged to Nora Halloran, a spoiled rich and aspiring girl. The Olivers are a respected Protestant family whose father is a land agent, a traditionally odious job to which he lends dignity and integrity in the carrying out of his business. There are two daughters, Mary and Jessie. The latter falls in love with Jim and Jim with her, and this love interest provides the main action of a very quiet, straightforward romantic novel which culminates in the mar- riage of Jim and Jessie. The secondary plot involves Sylvia Carew, Nora's aunt, who marries her old love, a former Protestant.

The book is dense with detail and well-written, showing a great advance over the earlier sketches. Her prose style is easy and flowing and her tone straightforward and honest. The characters are well-drawn, appealing, and fairly realistic, although not examined in any great depth. The plot is simple with a few twists and turns in the nature of a light and undramatic love story. In this early work, Tynan was well able to keep her plot line under control, leaving no loose ends. The plot arises quite naturally from the characters whom she introduces and the particular customs and beliefs current in the late nineteenth century.

There are two interesting features about Tynan's first novel, both closely related. The first is the relationship the book has to her own life. Written in the first year of Tynan's marriage, *The Way of a Maid* reflects the deep happiness and contentment which she experienced in her marriage. The book deals in a thematic way with the differences between steady, companion-able, and faithful love between the sexes both within and outside of marriage, and physical, passionate young love. Married love in general is her central theme in this novel, and she treats it with maturity and feeling. However, her own particular happiness seems to be at the basis of many of the statements in the book of which the following can be seen to be representative: "Earth has only one paradise and happy are they who enter at its gates. And within its garden spaces life blooms as a rose of many leaves. When God spake his sentence on the first man and woman He turned not away his face so as to forbid them love. There was never a work of His hands in the garden of life bloomed like that."[8]

Constrained by the late-Victorian sense of propriety of middle- and upper-class English and Irish ladies and, no doubt, by her own sense of modesty and reticence about sexual matters in keeping with her Catholic models, Tynan does not deal in this novel or in any of her novels with the physical aspects of love. She uses the conventions of the romantic novels to imply what could not be stated: girls blush, sigh, tremble, drop their eyes. Lovers, as she usually terms male suitors, pant, weep, and clasp girls to their chests as the girls swoon or fall. Despite these literary conventions, in this novel and in a number of others, there is still a sense of sincerity and honesty in Tynan's conviction that marriage was the preferable state for a woman and that the needs of women were fulfilled in marriage. These attitudes can be seen, not so much in a single novel, but in the novels taken as a body of work concerned with the central theme of love and marriage.

Many years later, in her autobiographical work *The Wandering Years,* she writes humorously and wryly of this particular feature of her work and her well-known discretion in her novels:

Arnold Bennet used to silence the discussion of unsavory topics when they arose: "Remember that Mrs. Tynan Hinkson is in the room."

I don't know why there was this tenderness to my susceptibilities, unless he meant to hint that my books were milk for babes. I, who had been adjured by friends in the 'nineties and since to let myself go, as though there was always *that* held back. It was no use telling them that I let go what I had. They used to shake their heads sorrowfully over me, and say that I had *It* right enough if only I would let myself go. I think in time they gave up thinking, or even suggesting, that I had *It.*[9]

Tynan had indeed let go in the matter which most counted with her, not physical passion for its own sake, but a sexual relationship which grew between man and woman, sanctioned by love in all its meanings of tenderness, affection, respect, shared companionship, and fully expressed in marriage and in the children of that marriage. Thus, in her novel and in her reminiscences about her personal friends, the greatest compliment she gives a woman, fictional or real, is that she had the rare gift of bringing order and tranquility into the lives of husband, children, and extended family of friends and relatives—the gift of establishing a home filled with love, caring, hospitality, and generosity, in which all members of the family could reach their individual potential.

Elaine Showalter's comments on the female English novelists apply equally to Katharine Tynan. She notes that the "Victorians expected women's novels to reflect the feminine values they exalted, although obviously the woman novelist herself had outgrown the constraining feminine role."[10] Tynan had led a full, creative life before she married. She had traveled, made many friends, published her work, and made money. She was independent and individualistic in all she did. Her marriage enhanced her life and gave her the additional roles of wife and mother. These new roles, with their duties and responsibilities, did not diminish her original role of writer and of friend to many people. In realistic terms she contributed much, financially, to her marriage and her work often enabled them to live in a gracious style, with the advantages of holidays abroad and help in the home. She lived a harmonious life, blending her many roles and succeeding in all of them. She falls into the third category of female novelists described by Showalter: "The third generation, born between 1840 and 1860, included sensation novelists and children's book writers. They seemed to cope effortlessly with the double roles of woman and professional, and to enjoy sexual fulfillment as well as literary success. Businesslike, unconventional, efficient, and productive, they moved into editorial and publishing positions as well as writing."[11]

Because of her own life experiences, Tynan knew that women could fulfill themselves with careers as well as through marriage and family life. It was important to Tynan to succeed in all three areas of her life. She had been alienated from her own mother whom she perceived as doing little more with her life than bearing children and "tending her brood." She was physically present in Tynan's life but offered little emotionally or intellectually. Tynan's career ambitions, although obviously in keeping with a strong desire to please her father, also reflected a more subconscious wish to be different from the woman she viewed as a personal failure. Tynan's perception of woman's role differed from the Victorian ideal of the Angel of the House in one significant way. She insisted on the importance of woman fulfilling herself as an individual. Only then could she be the kind of woman, mother, and wife who could draw out the best in husband, children, or friend. The autobiographical figure of Miss Katy in Tynan's late novel, *The Playground* (1930), illustrates in fiction the harmonious blending of roles in Tynan's own life.

Central to Tynan's thinking was her perception of the unique role women could play, a role which arose out of women's distinctly feminine attributes. The woman was the focal point of the home, inculcating in those around her the particular feminine wisdom of trust, gentleness, and understanding. She was a source of peace, a woman satisfied and fully developed in her own right who could, in turn, offer that self-confidence to others. The ability to love and the fortune to be well-loved are, in summary, the attributes of Tynan's ideal woman.

As is often the case with her writings, Tynan's poems reveal more of her feelings than her prose. An excerpt from a poem written some years after this first novel indicates her thinking about women's central role. Entitled "Any Woman" the first two stanzas read:

> I am the pillars of the house;
> The keystone of the arch am I.
> Take me away, and the roof and wall
> Would fall to ruin utterly.
>
> I am the fire upon the hearth,
> I am the light of the good sun,
> I am the heat that warms the earth,
> Which else were colder than a stone.

This poem goes on to elaborate maternal love in symbolic terms and clearly indicates Tynan's view of the role of women in the home. The following poem, although not indicated, possibly deals with the sad episode in her life following the successive deaths of her first two children. It is entitled "Any Wife":

> Nobody knows but you and I, my dear,
> And the stars, the spies of God, that lean and peer,
> Those nights when you and I in a narrow strait
> Were under the whips of God and desolate.
> In extreme pain, in uttermost agony,
> We bore the cross for each other, you and I,
> When, through the darkest hour, the night of dread,
> I suffered and you supported my head.
>
> Ties that bind us together for life and death,
> O hard-set fight in the darkness, shuddering breath,
> Because a man can only bear as he may,
> And find no tears for easing, the woman's way.
> Anguish of pity, sharp in the heart like a sword;
> Dost thou not know, O Lord? Thou knowest, Lord,
> What we endured for each other; our wounds were red
> When he suffered and I supported his head.
>
> Grief that binds us closer than smile or kiss,
> Into the pang God slips the exquisite bliss.
> You were my angel and I your angel, as he,
> The angel, comforted Christ in His Agony,
> Lifting Him up from the earth that his blood made wet,
> Pillowing the Holy Head, dabbled in sweat,
> Thou who were under the scourge knowest to prove
> Love by its pangs, love that endures for love.

This deeply personal poem in its intensity and honesty draws back a corner of the curtain on her married life which Tynan generally kept closed. Although obviously written from heartfelt

personal experience, she calls the poem "Any Wife" in order to
divert attention from the particular to that general experience
she shares with other women. The title implies that any woman
would do the same and, likewise, that any woman would
understand of what she speaks. The earlier poem, "Any Woman,"
serves the same function. She does not limit its interpretation by
calling the poem "Any Mother," but refers to all women who
have felt or will feel that intimacy of deeply shared sorrow and
suffering.

But these poems and feelings were to come at a later date in
her life. In her early novel one can see the first example of her
central theme of love and marriage that was to occupy nearly
every subsequent novel she was to write.

The second interesting feature of this novel is the treatment of
the traditional and historic Irish problem of the division that
existed between the Catholic majority and the Protestant
minority. Tynan is quite straightforward in acknowledging the
problem, and she deals openly with it in her novel. In fact, this
division between faiths is central to the plot, since the lovers
come from two different religious and social backgrounds. The
author writes that "The cleavage between Protestant and
Catholic in Coolevara, as elsewhere in Ireland, is incredibly
great. There is no common ground for these adherents of the
different religions to meet. . . ." However, their love, like that
of the lovers in her early poem "Puritan and Papist," overcomes
the religious difference.

In a passage early in the book the author gives her version of
the history of the inhabitants and of their religions. This passage
is also representative of her prose style throughout the novel:

The population is nearly altogether Catholic—sturdy, independent
folk, they are, for they have, most of them, a black drop in their veins
from one of Cromwell's Ironsides. Those inconquerable warriors
settled down in various parts of the fertile Irish country and, in days of
peace, had to ground arms before the violet-eyed daughters of the
mere Irish. In course of time they or their sons renegaded to the Scarlet
Woman, and became as sturdy on her side as they had been on the
other in their psalm-singing days. Admirable results these marriages
had. The men are great, brawny, square-shouldered giants, with a close
black thatch on their big heads and an infinite humour about the lines
of their close-shaven lips.[12]

Throughout the book she mentions the customs, occupations, and observances of both segments of the population, and she presents them without bias.

Like the predominant theme of love and marriage, the theme of religous differences also reflects Tynan's personal life. In the year in which she wrote the novel Tynan, too, had married a Protestant. Although there is no indication in her writings that this caused any comment or objection, she would have been aware that this was not usually done in the Irish society of her day. The only possible indication that the situation was a difficult one might be gleaned from the fact that she married in London, but her own description of her departure from Ireland would belie any serious objections:

On May 1st, 1893, I said good-bye to the old happy irresponsible life. I was going to London to be married and to settle there. I remember the last night at home. It was Sunday, and a great many people had come with good wishes and offerings, and it had been a very crowded and exciting day. I was going by the mail boat in the morning, which meant getting up very early. . . . I watched from the boat, as long as I could see it—my sight was better then than now—my father's figure in his whitish grey overcoat. He had walked to the end of the pier to see the last of me. I often wondered afterwards how I could have left him.[13]

Because of her own family background and her own experience in marrying a Protestant she was sensitive to the issues and problems this situation raised and, in her novels, consistently treats the relationship between members of the two faiths with tact and understanding. Tynan makes use of this secondary theme in many of her early novels, stressing the compatibility rather than the differences that could exist between the two religious sects. A loving and religious woman herself, she attempted in her novels to encourage the idea that Christianity could bring people together rather than drive them apart. Her own marriage was witness to the fact that she implemented her own beliefs in her actions.

II *Tynan's Continuing Career*

Tynan was well on the road to publishing her novels after her success with *The Way of a Maid*. In the same year she brought

out two more collections of sketches in the manner of the first.
An Isle in the Water (1895) contains the well written tale of the
supernatural, "The Death Spancel." Tales of the supernatural
was a mode for which Tynan had a real talent and which she
pursued in a number of her later novels. *A Land of Mist and
Mountain* (1895) contains more sketches of places and people
well known to her and which she fictionalizes to some extent.
Her second novel, *The Dear Irish Girl*, is set in Dublin and the
west of Ireland. Some of its action also takes place in London.
Over the years Tynan set approximately thirty of her novels and
almost all of her sketches in these two locations—Dublin and the
west. In a number of others the action takes place in equal
measure in Ireland and in England. Many of her later novels are
set on the Continent after World War I.

III   The Dear Irish Girl

Tynan's second novel has no reference to her personal life and
makes no reference to the existing religious differences in
Ireland. The novel shows Tynan beginning to distance herself
from her fiction and also beginning to incorporate more complex
plots, contemporary ideas, and a large cast of secondary
characters. The novel tells the story of Biddy O'Connor, a
motherless girl growing up in her father's house in fashionable
Merrion Square. Lovely and wayward, she flourishes under the
benevolent eye of her scholarly father, Dr. O'Connor, a
professor at nearby Trinity College. Through Carrie, her friend
across the Square, Biddy meets Maurice O'Hara, a young,
handsome, intelligent landlord of the Coolbawn estate in
Connemara. He and Dr. O'Connor share a mutual and scholarly
interest in the old Gaelic language and customs and together
pursue their studies and writing on the subject. Biddy falls in love
with Maurice and they reach an understanding while she and her
father are visiting his estate in the west of Ireland.

The segment of the novel which is set in Connemara gave
Tynan an opportunity to discuss through her fiction the kind of
interest and research in the Irish language which occupied such
friends as Douglas Hyde. It also gave her the occasion to
introduce minor characters, thumbnail sketches of interesting
types of Irish men and women. Among these are Maurice's old
nurse, Nannie; Lucy Hart, a strange, outspoken, masculine

woman who owns a large estate and who militantly fought the
Land League Movement; Eleanor Bingham, a neighbor, refined,
beautiful, and charitable. Tynan captures the dialect of the
country people in an exchange between Dr. O'Connor and Murty
O'Shaughnessy, an old retainer of the O'Hara family. The
passage is illustrative of Tynan's characteristic style and
portrayal of the rural people of Ireland:

"A malignant fairy would be rather a terrible creature, I suppose?" said
the doctor.
    "You may so, sir," said the old fellow, in evident good faith. "I've met
them on my road home at night many a time, an' a little distance off
'twould be a little thing like a withered leaf skippin' in your path, but as
you got nearer 'twould swell an' swell an' grow tall an' threatenin' like a
great tree on a mountain side. But I'm never afeared of them. I've the
words to put the fear in them. 'Lave me in pace,' I says, addressin' them
by name, an' makin' the sign fornint them, an' the things drifts off like a
mist, an' there I see the road in the moonlight before me, an' nothin' of
more harm upon it thin a playful lot of a mountain rabbit scuttin' into its
hole.[14]

    While the minor plot tells of the trials of Carrie, the major plot
line has Biddy leave Connemara believing that Maurice wishes to
marry Eleanor, his neighbor. On their return to Dublin, Dr.
O'Connor dies leaving Biddy unprovided for, because his stocks
in a bank are found to be worthless as the bank failed on the very
day of his death. Biddy is forced to go to London to live in misery
with her unfriendly aunt and her family. She believes Maurice to
be faithless because he did not come to Dublin for her beloved
father's funeral nor did he send a word of sympathy. She is
almost forced by circumstances to marry the marvelous Lon-
doner, Mr. Ayers, until an old friend of her father's, a widow who
had secretly loved him, finds her in London and takes her to the
South Seas. On her return to London, Mrs. Montague falls ill and
to please her, Biddy considers marriage to Mr. Ayers although
she does not love him. To contemplate her decision she takes a
walk in London, wanders into a bad area, is accosted by a group
of men and is rescued by a nurse dressed in black who turns out
to be Eleanor from Connemara. Eleanor explains that she did not
love Maurice, but was only a friend; that Maurice loved Biddy
and had not known of her father's death because he had been
called to America on that very day to deal with a discovery of oil

on some land in America which his mother did not know that she had owned. On his return he searched for Biddy, but by then she was in the South Seas where no one could write to her. Biddy says farewell to Mr. Ayers, returns to Dublin with Maurice, and is married there. They return to Connemara where old beloved servants and dogs await her. Mrs. Montague takes on the management of the house for the young bride, and Maurice's mother marries Eleanor's father in a happy ever after ending.

Unlike Tynan's first novel which has unity of time and place, a simple plot line and attention to character development, this second novel covers not only five locations but a considerable amount of time. The novel shows Tynan beginning to be attracted to the complicated plot and action of the popular romantic fiction of her day. At the point of natural conclusion, the agreement of Biddy and Maurice during her visit to Connemara, Tynan introduces an obstacle which only exists in the heroine's mind. The father's death is sudden and lamely explained. The long digression of the action in London and in the South Seas prolongs the solution. Finally, the coincidental and fortuitous meeting with Eleanor is in the nature of a deus ex machina leading to the final and happy resolution. The novel marks the beginning of Tynan's attempt to master the elements of popular novel writing for a mass audience. By her third novel, *She Walks in Beauty*, also published in 1899, it can be seen that she had struck upon a formula for writing light romantic novels, and, with slight variations depending on the exigencies of the individual plots, this formula was to succeed for her during the years up to and including the years of World War I.

IV   She Walks in Beauty

She Walks in Beauty, published in London in 1899 and in America in 1900, exhibits the first of her long and complicated plots filled with countless characters. Briefly, the story tells of a Mr. Graydon, an Irishman living in the west of Ireland who does private tutoring for boys resident in his home. A dignified, quiet, scholarly man, he is poor but totally dedicated to his profession of preparing each individual boy for college and for life. A widower, he lives a peaceful life with his daughters Pamela and Sylvia. The opening chapters of the book certainly parallel

Tynan's own experience as a young girl living on her father's farm.

The young Sir Anthony Trevithick, an Englishman and son of an old friend of Mr. Graydon's, is staying in the house as a pupil, and the story recounts his falling in love with the pretty, gentle Pamela. As the romance progresses it becomes apparent that Lady Jane Trevithick secretly hates Mr. Graydon and Pamela because of her own early disappointment in love. She discourages Pamela from loving her son under the guise of kindness and generosity, and she convinces her that her son loves an English girl named Kitty. Kitty however is secretly in love with Anthony's best friend, Captain Leslie. Anthony is called away and asks his mother to mail a letter to Mr. Graydon stating his intentions to marry his daughter. The letter is never sent and Pamela, broken-hearted and ashamed, returns to Ireland convinced that Anthony does not love her and has, in fact, jilted her. Lonely, embarassed by her broken engagement, and distressed by her father's fast failing health due to overwork and poverty, she becomes engaged to a much older, kind, wealthy Lord Glengall in order to remedy her own and her father's situation. Anthony returns in time to rectify matters and marries Pamela. Her sister, Sylvia, an independent girl who had secretly loved Lord Gengall, marries him, and in the meanwhile, through the secondary plot, she inherits great wealth on the death of Miss Spencer, an old spinster and dear friend. Anthony and Mr. Graydon are reconciled to Lady Jane; Kitty marries her captain; finally, Mr. Graydon is at last free to write the scholarly book he had planned all his life. The story ends with the marriage or engagements of all the various characters in the traditional manner of comedy.

The plot is impelled along its path by the romantic attachments of the various characters and the happy resolution of these love affairs. The theme, however, explores in a light way the relationship between father and daughter—the mutual affection, respect, and loyalty that exists between Pamela and her father. The comradeship and companionship portrayed in this fictional relationship mirror that which Tynan shared with her own father. The reader can also detect in the unusual relationship between young Sylvia and the older Glengall a variation on the same theme. Their relationship is paternal and filial rather than romantic. It can also be seen in this novel that the intense relationship between father and daughters influenced their decision regarding the type of man each wished to marry, and each hopes to find in her husband those qualities so admired in their father. The influence of Tynan's own experience is more marked in this novel than in most of her others. However, it is possible to identify many of her own father's characteristics in the many father figures which fill her novels. Her father was a dominant and unforgettable personality, and in her novels Tynan was able to draw on her knowledge of his dynamic character.

V   The Formula of the Novels

The formula which Tynan found so useful for her purposes begins to emerge in her third novel. The pattern she established includes the following elements: a major plot line that deals with the central romance between a young, inexperienced poor girl from a good family of either a noble line in declining circumstances or an old family line which has suffered because of religious reasons. She loves, and is loved by, a young, refined, often wealthy, and high-born young man. The course of this romance does not run smoothly because of the interference of one or both of the families and because of misunderstandings on the part of the lovers themselves developing out of shyness or a sense of unworthiness. These romances invariably end happily with the marriages of the major and minor characters. The secondary plot generally involves a love affair, but one which is much less complicated. It is in the secondary plot that Katharine Tynan introduces any colorful, eccentric, or strange characters, and these are presented as caricatures. Her major characters are seldom fully developed and are often merely representatives of sets of virtues or vices. However, she never introduces a truly evil or corrupt character in the early novels. Occasionally characters appear to be so, but Tynan always finds a redeeming quality in their lives or in the manner of their dying, and she often provides sound extenuating circumstance, influences, or psychological reasons for their behavior. Thus, no one is ever so bad that the author cannot find reasons or excuses.

Tynan enjoyed writing about the upper class and their social manners and customs. Her books always describe dress and food with great relish. Her young male leading characters are uniformly brave, handsome, courageous, generous, sensitive, refined, and gentle. Tynan also enjoyed giving them resounding and lengthy names calculated to indicate their high birth. Her female characters fall into the general categories exhibited in this novel. They are either gentle, shy, refined, and unworldly, or young, attractive, strong-willed, and highly principled. The older women are often unmarried or widowed, wise, and wealthy. Of the minor female characters, these can be troubled, jealous, vain, selfish, or insensitive. Often the family relationships, as in *She Walks in Beauty,* are set up in such a way that the leading female characters are the daughters of a widower and the young men are the sons of strong mothers with weak or absent husbands. The young heroes of the novels exhibit the characteristics that met the Victorian definition of manliness. Adventurous, they love both sport and animals; attractive and handsome, they sublimate their sexual energy into modified modern "quests." The heroines fall into either one or the other of the traditional comic categories: the virginal type and the marriageable.

In terms of both characterization and plot, Tynan's romantic novels follow in the tradition of the comic story of which Northrop Frye writes: "Its themes often feature disguise and concealment of identity, both from other characters and from the audience, and its plot normally moves toward an end acceptable to the audience but unlikely under the conditions of the action, so that some surprising or unexpected event is needed to resolve the conclusion."[15] Tynan had quickly and easily mastered the elements of formulaic fiction made available to her both in traditional romantic and comic stories and in the novels written by women of her own generation. Elaine Showalter writes that the "success of the women novelists and the ease with which they wrote resulted from the happy correspondence between the message they wished to communicate and the extreme stylization of the sensation novel, a genre in which everything that was not forbidden was compulsory."[16]

Working within the stylized structure of the romantic novel of the late nineteenth century, Tynan communicated the message that women were resourceful, energetic, lovable, and although they were often the victim of circumstances, society, or one another, true love had a way of winning out. The happy ending motif allowed Tynan to present her readers with a certain amount of escapist fantasy which they could enjoy after enduring with the heroines the trials and tribulations of late Victorian life. In addition, her novels had an appeal for her English readers because she introduced beautiful and mysterious Irish settings, quaint, secondary Irish characters, and intriguing descriptions of those strange Catholic institutions—the convents. Tynan, however, cognizant of her audience, only presented these "Irish" features within a context readily understood by her readers. The action of the novels takes place always within the realm of Victorian English modes of manners and behavior. The major characters, particularly the men, are always aristocratic or upper class. The framework of these novels, which are acceptable to the Victorian English woman, allows for the introduction of, but not the focusing on, Irish elements.

John Cawelti in his recent study of formulaic fiction suggests four hypotheses regarding formulaic literature[17] which, when applied to Tynan's novels, illustrate how fully in command of the formula she was. Tynan's novels, like formula stories, affirmed the current Victorian attitudes and ideas by recreating a world within those Victorian strictures. In line with this, the novels resolve the tensions inherent in Victorian, and later, in modern society by expressing in fiction ideas which were current but unexpressed or repressed by society. This release of tension works toward the continuity of the culture which created the tension because it allows for the outlet of emotion. Likewise, Tynan's novels allow for the exploration of the forbidden, in this case, the mild sexual exploits and love affairs of her heroes and heroines. Finally, the novels, particularly the postwar novels, like formula stories in general, assist in the assimilation of new ways of life into the old former ways of life.

In keeping with Cawelti's further elaboration of the genre of romance as a formula pattern,[18] Tynan's novels meet the definition, in that they are organized around a love relationship and have as a moral the triumph of love and the sacredness of marriage. Her novels, from their earliest beginnings to the last semirealistic novels of her postwar period, were to pursue the theme of love which would win out in the end and the theme of monogamous marriage as the true and worthiest estate.

VI Julia: *A Representative Novel Set in Ireland*

One of Tynan's novels set in Ireland reflects her manipulation of the elements available to her in the various traditions with which she was familiar. It exhibits features of the Irish tradition as outlined by Flanagan; features of the tradition of the English popular novel; and, finally, the elements of formulaic fiction as suggested by Cawelti. *Julia,* published in 1904, tells the story of Julia, one of six daughters of Denis Driscoll MacCormac O'Kavanagh of Kerry, all rosy milkmaids except for Julia, the ugly duckling with yellow skin and dark hair. They are farmers who retained their Catholic faith in an earlier generation and who, as a result, lost their lands and property.

The dominant member of the family is the grandmother, Mrs. O'Kavanagh, who, conscious of their noble antecedents, finds in Julia, her favorite, the qualities of race and breeding and of blood which signify that she, like a young thoroughbred horse, belongs to a different class from her common sisters. This family is related to Sir Jasper O'Kavanagh, a Protestant landowner, who inherited all the family property on his side. His grandnephew, Mortimer, returns after an English education, to manage the estate and he falls in love with Julia, his cousin. Following the usual complications of Tynan's plotting, Mortimer is called away from the village and gossip ruins Julia's reputation. Urged by her own desire for a vocation and her grandmother's wishes, Julia enters a convent. Mortimer views this on his return as a form of living death, but he visits her in the convent and sees its beauty and appeal. He proposes marriage and Julia realizes her true calling is not in the convent. They marry with the permission of an enlightened priest at the end of the novel. The happy conclusion rests in the uniting of the two branches of an old family—Protestant and Catholic—the uniting of the lands and property and the restoration of a Catholic mistress, Julia, to the old ancestral home. The secondary plot deals with the theme of the absentee landlords in a small way and with the love affairs of numerous secondary characters.

One can see in this novel Tynan's predilection for writing about the upper class and about the idea that blood will always tell no matter how circumstances change the status of the characters. There is an affinity between the young Mortimer and the farmer's family: he is made welcome by them because of his station in life; he in turn admires their simple way of life, their health, pleasures, and attitudes. He bestows on them the dignity of his presence and is paid in turn with rural wisdom. Both sets of characters are equally idealized; both exhibit the stereotypical characteristics of their classes.

The happy union at the end of the novel between the Protestant Mortimer and the Catholic Julia is a device which Tynan often used in her novels set in Ireland. The marriage of two members of the different faiths as the happy conclusion to the action of these novels points to Tynan's own enlightenment and spirit of tolerance. However, the novels do not examine in any great depth the realities of the religious situation in Ireland. Tynan does not explain the difficulties in the way of a mixed marriage nor how permission or dispensations were given. She conveniently ends most of these stories with the marriage and, therefore, does not have to deal with the social consequences of mixed marriage in Ireland, or the problems which would arise if there were any children of the marriage.

VII   The Novels Set in England

In the novels written at the same period which Tynan set in England, she avoids the subject of religion entirely. She was increasingly to locate her novels in England and for a very particular reason.

As early as 1891 both Tynan and Yeats were well aware of the necessity of finding an English audience and market for their work. Yeats wrote to advise her on this matter, telling her to remember that by being as Irish as she could be in her writing she would be both more original and true to herself, and "in the long run, more interesting, even to an English audience."[19] Although Tynan agreed with this statement in terms of poetry at the beginning of her career, her experience in prose writing had taught her otherwise. She wrote poetry for its own sake, but she wrote her novels for money, and she came to know her market— a knowledge illustrated in the following passage, written at the time of the writing of her third novel:

. . . the race of Irish readers of Irish books is not yet, and the more Irish we are the less likely we are to find favour with English readers.

. . . The English indeed liked Lever. . . . Ladies who write in the same light-hearted and irresponsible fashion are sure of their vogue. But give them a microcosm of the Irish nature as the Irish know it, consciously or unconsciously, and it is worse to them than a Chinese puzzle.[20]

She followed her own dicta, and the light romantic novels she wrote were to be set more often in England or on the Continent than in Ireland. She always managed to retain the Irish interest by including secondary characters of Irish birth or descent in her stories, or by setting the action equally in both countries.

VIII   Oh, What A Plague Is Love

Oh, What A Plague Is Love, published in 1896, is entirely set in England on the lovely estate of an upper-class English family. In Tynan's now standard opening line she introduces the reader to the central male character, in this case, Charles Frederick Marmaduke Strangways.

This plot epitomizes Tynan's standard plots for the novels set in England. In it, the common elements are the widower father of daughters and sons, a man who periodically falls in love with the women he meets in society; one of his sons, an impetuous, feckless, passionate youth; spinster sisters, prosperous widow, and friendless girl. These characters recur in her novels like the members of a repertory company appearing under various names, and involved in complex plots which inevitably result in happy marriages. One further element which Tynan introduces in the novel and which she was to use repeatedly to the end of her career is the picture of charming old age, generally embodied in a wealthy widow of great experience and social wisdom, beloved, respected, and influential in her small social circle of manor house and country town.

IX   A Red, Red Rose

A Red, Red Rose (1903) is also entirely set in England and introduces the first of the international sets of characters in Tynan's novels. In this case, they are Tom and Amelia Brent, two wealthy young Americans. Amelia is elegant, exquisitely dressed, gay, open, and blunt. Her brother Tom is a quiet Harvard man, humorous, and a true gentleman. They buy Oriels, an English manor house that once belonged to the St. Denises, who are descended from the Fitzgeralds of Ireland. Amelia falls in love with the handsome, poverty stricken Hilary St. Denis and eventually marries him after many complications. Tom falls in love with a sweet local girl, Peggy Searle, a parson's daughter. She is linked by her mother who is socially ambitious, to her unpleasant cousin Fred Grace whose family has money and position. In the course of the novel it is revealed that her mother has been blackmailed because of an early indiscretion into promising her beautiful daughter to Fred Grace. Peggy dislikes her mother and pities her. She is only happy in company with her father whom she loves and idolizes. The emotion is mutual, and the relationship between Peggy and Cuthbert Searle is one of the more interesting features in the book because of its intensity and exclusivity. Eventually Tom Brent perseveres, pays off the blackmail, frees Mrs. Searle from her promise, and woos and wins Peggy whom he marries at the end of the book.

As can be seen from these two early novels, Tynan was tailoring her settings, characterization, and themes to suit her audience. She was gradually to abandon substantial issues to focus almost exclusively on love relationships of various kinds, father and daughter, girl and suitor, lover and girl. She was to set her novels not only more often in England but in an indeterminate time and place that allowed for maximum manipulation of the relationships with little reference to the external world of reality. The English novels, even more than her Irish novels, present females in limited roles and provide escapist fantasy for her feminine audience of the time.

X *Summary*

In summary, then, it is not necessary to examine each novel Tynan produced in this genre of light romantic fiction, written before the war, to realize that she had found a workable formula which made use of traditional elements found in Irish fiction and, also, her own personal experience. Although admiring Irish writers such as Edgeworth and English writers such as Austen, Tynan had little desire to write novels that seriously examined the two societies in which she lived. Although reflecting elements of the two cultures, her novels cannot be read as social documents except in the broadest sense. Her novels idealize the upper class and romanticize the peasant class, and make use of stock characters from both classes with easily recognizable attributes.

She enjoyed the writing of these novels, in much the same way as her readers enjoyed them. She created a little region for others and herself to wander in, tinged with some reality, taking note of some social or religious issues. She created a happy world of love and marriage, adventure, balls, parties, food and drink, with enough realistic detail to engage the interest of the contemporary reader, knowledgeable, or hoping to be knowledgeable, about fashion or society.

Her plots are intriguingly complicated and move with lightning speed, the impetus always being the happy union of two star-crossed lovers. Her language is kept simple and frank, and her ear for dialogue, in particular Irish conversation, is often very good. Her prose style is in keeping with her subject matter, dependent on periodic sentences and an easy flowing rhythm which makes the writing eminently readable.

Through Tynan's awareness of her audience, her estimation and understanding of the English market, and her early experience in journalism and sketch writing, she came to have a keen grasp of her situation. Almost intuitively she had begun to write novels which were to fall readily into formulaic patterns. Encouraged by her success, needing money, conscious of her limitations as a novelist, and possessing the requisite skills of a highly fertile imagination, an easy, readable prose style, and a true sense for the tastes of her readers, Tynan turned her talents to producing highly successful romances. These entailed all the features of the traditional comic mode, the newer features of formulaic writing, and at the same time, retained certain features of the Irish novel tradition. It was, in her time, a unique combination of traditions and talents which allowed Tynan to achieve great success in the single fiction genre to which she turned her hand in the years dating from her marriage to the beginning of World War I. The war years and her husband's death marked a watershed in her poetic career and in her novel writing career as well. The postwar novels, to be discussed in the final chapter, still followed in the romantic mode, but Tynan did attempt forays into other modes as well. However, in the final analysis it was the formula romantic story which was to serve her well both in her early and in her later career.

CHAPTER 8

The Final Years

A FTER her husband's death in January, 1919, Tynan spent long periods in England, renewing old friendships, traveling, and writing. Eventually, she decided to travel to Germany, and she recorded her impressions and experiences in her book, *Life in the Occupied Area*, published in 1925. One of Tynan's sons had been stationed in Germany at the end of the war, and his vivid, firsthand accounts and descriptions had sparked her interest in the country where her husband had studied many years before. Free to travel, she undertook her journey with enthusiasm. Another factor in her decision to see Germany at this time was financial. The German economy at the end of the war was in chaos, and the foreign visitor with a more stable currency could live cheaply and well.

Tynan's desire to live in a manner and style to which she had become accustomed runs as a leitmotiv in her writings after the war. In Europe the war had disrupted the fabric of life with which she was familiar. With the death of her husband and the breakup of that family life around which her own life had truly centered, her emotional and financial circumstances were also disrupted.

The trip to Germany, then, was both a change of scene for her and an opportunity to live for a while, at least, with some graciousness and ease. She continued to live and expect others to live in a world which no longer existed—a world of servants and comforts, a world in which society was governed by class consciousness, and where people recognized their station in life and behaved accordingly. What Tynan did not realize was that that society had been destroyed in the war. The foundations of that class system had been altered forever by the war and its aftermath. When the consequences of this social upheaval were brought home to Tynan in her daily life, she resented its actuality and rejected it.

After her arrival in Germany, Tynan settled easily into life in Cologne, and once she found suitable lodgings, her life assumed a pattern which allowed her to work

. . . with an incredible ease and rapidity and joy in the working. Every time I sat to work I was conscious of an inner warm pleasure in what I was going to do. Between July, 1922, and May, 1923, inclusive I wrote without effort and with sheer joy in the doing, three novels, a play, a book of "Memories" of dead friends, and the book that is under your eyes. I was doing constant journalism as well and short stories, verse and writing a great many letters.[1]

The remarkable feature in this statement is the joy with which she worked. Her husband had died in 1919, and in 1923 she had been on the move constantly for four years with no fixed home. Yet, here she is in Germany, able to write, to function, to support herself and live well. She was sixty-three years old.

Despite Tynan's enthusiasm and facility in writing at this time, *Life in the Occupied Area* is possibly the weakest book in her large corpus. It shows the signs of hasty composition and the naiveté of its author. The book offers easy solutions to the problems of Europe after the war: the recreation of the shattered world in the image of Tynan's prewar society. Tynan's advice and recommendations in this book are unrealistic, if hopeful. Her failure to grasp the fact that the world her generation had made and known was gone and her rejection of the world that took its place, perforce limits critical appraisal of her thought and work. Nearly a decade of writing was left to Tynan, and her ideas and preferences were to remain relatively unchanged during that time. However, she was well aware of the needs and desires of her readers. If she hoped to continue to succeed financially, it was necessary for Tynan to produce novels which would appeal to the audience of women readers after the war. The novels which date from this period reflect the ambivalence of both Tynan and her audience. Many of the novels are dateless, in that they are set in an indeterminate time period, in rural areas of England, and deal with domestic situations and love triangles. These novels could as easily have been written before the war. Timeless in nature, they offered a form of escapism and entertainment to the reader.

Despite Tynan's obvious predilection for writing novels which dealt with a past that was comfortable and familiar, she did attempt to include elements of contemporary culture in a number of the later novels. One theme, developed in her war poems and used in the novels she wrote following the end of the war, concerned those girls who never had an opportunity to get married because the men of their generation had been killed. In those poems with this theme she is able to offer little consolation, and in a poem such as "The Vestal" she describes such a girl. The function of these poems and those sections of her novels which discuss the conditions and circumstances of these girls seems to be to call the attention and sympathy of the reader to their lonely and often thwarted lives. These women of whom she writes are those girls who never had a lover, never had a chance to fall in love, to enjoy themselves at dances and parties as girls had in that world before 1914. They had not had the chance to be gay, girlish, and carefree, and Tynan pities them, because the normal course of their lives had been altered forever. She pities them more than she pities those who had lost loved ones in death because they, at least, had known love and passion: they had someone to mourn. They had children to live for and memories to sustain them. Their sacrifice and suffering had ennobled them and given them dignity.

As has been mentioned, Tynan defined herself in terms of her relationship with others; she had been daughter, wife, mother, and friend. It is clear in her writing on the subject, that the figure of the woman unfulfilled by a marital relationship filled her with pity. Although the war poems evince little anger, given their nature and purpose, she was not so constrained in her novels. In these she grieves that society has been so changed. She mildly criticizes those former soldiers who married girls younger than themselves, neglecting the girls who had lived through the war, their own generation, who could not compete with the younger and more modern girls of the early 1920s. She criticizes the government, too, for not providing enough jobs for the ex-servicemen in England, and indirectly, causing many of them to emigrate to find work. Characters in her postwar novels are often the mouthpieces for these sentiments.

Another sentiment so expressed in the war poetry and in the novels which deal with the war, reflects the feelings of all those involved in the war. The man who had fought had little time for the man who had not. The family who had lost a member felt hostility toward families who had not. Loss created a common bond, as did suffering. Tynan had shared in that suffering, and she herself had experienced the gulf that divided those who had suffered from those who had not. They were of the company, the inner circle, and her novels of the period address those who wore the badge of suffering; they reflect the divisions in society after the war.

I The Realistic Novels

Tynan disliked many features of modern English life and longed for a return to former days. Acknowledging this could never be, she creates for herself a new fictional world in much the same way she had created, earlier in her career, a world of escapism. The realities of London were too pressing to be ignored and her audience was changing. Her readers were no longer the women of leisure of the middle and upper classes, desirous of reading about a world very similar to their own. Now her readers came from all classes, the women who had survived the war, and lived and worked in London, and for them Tynan had to write about their London. The reality of the lives of the shop girls, office workers, and unmarried lonely women impressed Tynan, and in her fictional world she acknowledged and then provided remedies for harsh reality. She would, if she could, have created a utopia for them; in any event, sincerity, if not practicality, lies behind many of these novels. The novels to be discussed will serve to illustrate this particular fictional world which Tynan created in her postwar novels.

II The Rich Man

The Rich Man (1929) tells of Captain Christopher Delaray Robinson, a former soldier, returning to England after the war and seeking something to do with his life. He is the son of a wealthy man, a member of the new class of rich entrepreneurs who were gradually replacing the men of inherited wealth. Mr. Robinson's wealth is reprehensible to his son. By an accident of fate the son meets a beautiful young girl whose mother does typing for a livelihood. Through association with these genteel women he enters the world of London which is filled with suffering poor, the ill, the unemployed, the overworked, the exploited, and the lonely. All of these categories are individually represented in the various characters Captain Robinson meets. As background to the action the author describes the killing pollution, the poor housing, the incipient cooperative societies. Captain Robinson finds a true and worthy cause for which he can use his vast wealth, inherited from his father who dies nobly, without naming the insane young Irish man who murdered him.

Captain Robinson appears like an angel of mercy throughout the book, fulfilling every need and lowly wish of the people he encounters. Totally enlightened, completely generous, and immensely wealthy, he single-handedly rescues hundreds. And, too, he is at all times filled with modesty, dignity, and insight; he is shy, sensitive, and full of self-abnegation and the guilt that his great good fortune causes him. The book is one long wish-fulfillment—Tynan's vision of how such troubling social problems could be solved. It is an escapist fantasy for herself and the girls she saw trapped in the urban prison of modern London, far from the joys of health, of free countryside, of nature, of love, marriage, and children.

III   Haroun of London

Haroun of London (1927) is a novel in the same vein as *The Rich Man*, although in this case, the angel of mercy, Mr. Smith, is an older man with no wish to marry nor to be known by his beneficiaries. Motivated by a memory of his mother, he wishes to relieve suffering whenever he finds it. Unlike the younger Captain Robinson, Mr. Smith is a hardheaded businessman, and his generosity takes more practical forms. However, the plot moves ahead through Mr. Smith's encounters with various characters who are ciphers for the problems each represents. As a result, as in the earlier book, there is little or no character development. This is made obvious in the abrupt ending. Having taken the action of the plot as far as she could, Tynan ends abruptly with Smith's sudden death from a chill which he caught on Christmas Eve distributing hampers of food in the slums of London.

The novels which Tynan wrote using the device of the rich man operating in secret to relieve suffering and to bestow health, wealth, and happiness on the unfortunate working poor of the London suburbs differ from her formulaic romantic novels in that they are episodic. These novels deal with the fates of many different characters within the story, and do not always end with a happy marriage as resolution of the action.

IV   The Man from Australia

While the majority of Tynan's novels written after the war were set in England and incorporated features of English life into their stories, Tynan did continue to write novels set in Ireland. These Irish novels seldom deal with contemporary urban life in Ireland nor do they confront any political or social issues. In *The Man from Australia*, however, Tynan makes use of the device she was using in her English novels of the same period. John Darling, the leading male character, makes a fortune in Australia and comes to Ireland to seek his only living relatives, his distant cousins. They are living in an old, decaying, great house in the Irish countryside, and the novel tells of Darling's rescue of his female cousins, their parents, neighbors, and friends in various ways through his financial generosity and moral character. This novel is not episodic, however, and the plot line follows the love story of John and his beautiful mysterious cousin Aileen and ends with their gloriously happy marriage.

V   Grayson's Girl

In the novels which Tynan set in England and which offer utopian solutions to real problems she began to come near to a form of realism in her writing. In a series of companion stories Tynan attempted, not too successfully, to write novels of realism. These are not episodic in structure but are developed on the traditional lines of the novel and hold in common a number of recurring characters. *The Lover of Women* (1928) introduces the reader to Simon Grayson, called a lover of women, "because of his service and devotion to women" and tells of his services in detail. *Grayson's Girl* (1930) takes up his story and carries it through the story of his only child, a daughter. Simon owns a draper's shop in London, and his life is the life of the petit bourgeoisie, a class with which Tynan seldom concerned herself. Simon meets Mr. William Peters, who owns a famous shop in London's Oxford Street. He, as well as Simon, is a recurring character in the novels, and through these two men Tynan examines the new class of working men and women who appeared after the war; the spread of sprawling suburbs; the cooperative movement. These realistic and significant issues are looked at through the relationships of the various characters who become friends or partners or lovers. The story focuses on Rose, Grayson's daughter, who becomes relatively emancipated after the war and integrally involved both in business and in social issues. She marries at the end of the story, but the implication in this novel of realism is that she will return to her work and that perhaps her daughter will carry on in the tradition of the Grayson family.

VI   The Playground

One final book which Tynan wrote in this vein of tempered realism was the long and diffuse novel called *The Playground* (1930). The story opens in the slums of Dublin in the late nineteenth century. John Tracey is a little boy living with poor parents and a number of brothers and sisters. His father occasionally works as a carpenter, and John goes with his father to Glenmalure, a thinly disguised picture of Tynan's home at Whitehall. There he meets Mr. Barton, a character closely modeled on Mr. Andrew Tynan, and Katy, his daughter, who is closely modeled on Katharine Tynan herself.

John Tracey, as a child, learns to love the beautiful country and longs for his beloved sister, who is a cripple, to be able to visit the country. He wishes that there was a park or playground near the slum where they could carry her and allow her to enjoy the sun and air. The sister dies, and John is fired by a promise he made to her to provide a playground in the slum. His father dies and he goes to live with the Bartons who undertake his education. His mother and brothers remain in Dublin, but as John grows older he is sent to an English public school and then abroad to acquire knowledge of gardening. He works for the Formosa Nurseries in England and falls in love with Lord Dent's daughter, Marjorie. They settle in England and in 1914, when he is thirty years old, he enlists in the army, goes to the war, is wounded, and sent home.

Meanwhile his brothers, who attended Pearse's school in Dublin, are portrayed as having been radicalized by knowing both Padraic Pearse and Thomas MacDonagh, actual Irish patriots who were executed following the 1916 Rising. These brothers join the Irish political movement in Dublin, and this act splits the family, since John continues to live in England and remains loyal to his adopted country. The brothers and the Sinn Fein movement are not presented sympathetically in the course of the novel in comparison with the portrayal of John Tracey. However, at the end of the war the family is reunited. Fergus, John's brother, gives up politics and comes to work in a garden. Pierce, another brother, leaves Ireland for Oxford. Thus the Sinn Feiners are portrayed as giving up their fight for Ireland.

John visits Ireland and, having met the ubiquitous Mr. William Peters who had opened a huge playground in England, is inspired to do the same in Dublin. In a weak falling off of the plot, John meets Lady Cromar who owns a park which she has tried to maintain for the children over the years. Now old and lacking in money, she gladly hands over the park to John, and the novel ends with the reuniting of a secondary character, George, an English gentleman, with his Irish daughter-in-law whose husband had been killed in the war.

The plot of the novel is too ambitious, and the many shifts of scene and the many incidents swamp Tynan's intentions. One of the last books she was to write, it is important for her portrayal, after many years, of herself, her father, and her home at Whitehall. It is also important for her attempt to weave into the action of the novel set in England references to the political situations in Ireland. But owing to her decision not to deal with political action or violence, her portrayal of the Irish aspect is weak and vague. The resolution of the conflict within the Tracey family, by which she indicates the conflict between the Irish and the English, is weak and unrealistic and hints at her personal opinions.

In those novels which dealt in any realistic way with the Irish following World War I, in which many Irish fought for England, and following the political upheaval during the establishment of the Free State and the Irish Republic, Tynan is inclined to have her Irish characters well developed in the early stages of the book, to portray rural Ireland in realistic terms, and then to shift the focus. She impels her characters, as in this novel and others such as *Connor's Wood* (1933), to leave Ireland and travel to France in particular, or to England, to pursue their education or their careers. It seems, in retrospect, an effort on the author's part to avoid dealing with the modern Ireland she was watching develop and which did not always please her politically or emotionally.

Tynan's move to realism in her postwar novels was dictated less by choice than by her changing audience. Realism in any form had not been an interest of Tynan's in her early fiction nor was she inclined to it by her nature. Like politics, social problems on a large scale and social movements involving the masses, did not capture her creative interest. In her novels as in her poetry, she was concerned with the individual, not the group. Her strength lay in her vivid imagination and her interest in manners and mores, and consequently, she was unable and, indeed, unwilling to deal with the larger panorama of a society in upheaval. Thus her novels of realism do not stand, as others of the period stand, as social documents. Nor do they stand among her more entertaining novels. They are, however, evidence of her willingness to alter her style and her mode to suit a new audience.

VII   Novels About Women

In the altered society of the postwar era, Tynan was forced to update her plots and characters. Although disinclined to accept the changes wrought in the status of women, she was forced to deal with the changing roles and social behavior of the modern woman in her novels. The books under discussion here sum up Tynan's efforts to incorporate into her fiction the social changes she observed around her, and, at the same time, her efforts to maintain that fictional world in which she had become comfortable.

VIII   An International Marriage

An International Marriage (1933) is a very long novel with a more complicated plot than those mentioned previously. Its action spans many years, covering the periods before, during, and after the war. The story tells of Miss Amelia, a wealthy and parentless lady of the manor in a lovely English village, who remains single until early middle age. Mr. Donne is her agent and lawyer, and his wife takes a maternal interest in Amelia's life. Amelia lives in a beautiful house and has a constant suitor and friend in the spiritual Mr. Southwell, an Anglican clergyman, who, eventually, converts to Catholicism and maintains his celibate life in the church.

The novel depicts the effect of the war years on the village and the involvement of the women in war work while their men were away. Following Amelia's intensive work which finished with the end of the war, she travels to Vienna where she meets a much younger man, Franz Von Ludolph, an Austrian nobleman, who had suffered greatly in the war—on the other side. A Catholic and a member of the enemy forces, he, nevertheless, appeals greatly to Amelia, and she marries him and returns to her village. The village greets the marriage with some ridicule, but this is overcome by the influential Lady Marcia, the wealthy elderly lady of the manor, closely modeled on one of Tynan's English friends.

Franz overcomes the hostility of the local people by his personality, charm, and manners. They live happily for some time and Amelia bears a son, an event which completes her happiness. However, she senses Franz's boredom and enforced idleness and, as a gift, pays to have his family castle in the Tyrol restored. Franz is delighted to return with his family and his compatriots in the war, but Amelia, pregnant and lonely, becomes homesick for England. The secondary plot which involves the mad friend Stefan reveals that both Stefan and Franz had suffered horribly in Russia where Franz had fallen in love with Nada, a Russian girl, who had helped them. Both men leave to seek the girl but Nada eventually finds her own way to the castle, only to die. Amelia is reassured concerning Franz's love for her with the birth of their second child, but Stefan, who in his madness blames Amelia for Franz's loss of Nada, breaks into her room and in the ensuing struggle, his gun goes off and Franz is killed. Stefan, too, dies, having run away and fallen off a cliff in his grief. Amelia is grief-stricken and resolves to divide her time between Austria and England and ends with the promise of more chapters of her story.

In this novel Tynan retained her interest in the marriage between Protestant and Catholic, and in portraying the English upper class. She deals with the issue of the war not so much in her narrative as through the characters of the men who had suffered and survived the war, and in the actions of the villagers. The book also touches on a modern theme in its examination of

the marriage of an older woman and a younger man. More frank
than many of her books, it includes Mrs. Donne's conversations
with Amelia about her appearance, dress, and underwear. Mrs.
Donne insists that Amelia must remain young, fit, and beautifully
dressed to retain her husband's interest. At the end, Amelia is
well able to endure the loss of her adored husband because she
can content herself with her memories. She does not have to fear
the end of the idyll because her husband died before she could
grow old and ugly. Because of his early death, her romance
remained intact and untouched, and she had her beloved
children to live for. Despite incorporating modern themes and
features, Tynan's book is once again swamped by the complicated plot line and by the unattractive nature of her leading
character.

IX   The Respectable Lady

One of her last attempts at writing a modern novel is the book
entitled *The Respectable Lady* (1927). In this book she has the
most surprising twist of her many plots, because in it the
respectable lady of the title lives with a man who is not her
husband and both have living spouses. This amazing relationship
is not revealed until the very end of the story which, throughout,
deals with the absolute perfection of Mrs. Heseltine's outward
life, manners, dress, and social behavior. Miss Simmons accidentally discovers the secret and muses about Sir John, Mrs.
Heseltine's real husband:

She prided herself simply on being a woman of the world and she knew
Sir John Evelyn by repute. He was a man wrapped up in his library
when he was not busy with politics, always attending book sales, a
scholar, elderly, not the man to keep a woman like Mrs. Heseltine, in
whom Miss Simmons dimly recognized a passionate woman under the
cold exterior. When other people talked of Mrs. Heseltine's nun-like
appearance, Miss Simmons had remembered a curve of the nostrils, a
thrill in the voice. And Ralph Heseltine. The man was not worth it, but
very often men who were not worth it had swept women off their feet.[2]

In the conclusion of the novel, Mrs. Heseltine explains to her
friend Diana, that her immense respectability had been an
attempt to make up for that fatal mistake of leaving her husband
and children and causing Ralph to leave his. Ralph leaves her
eventually because she could not compensate for the loss of

softness, comfort, and warmth that he had found in his own wife and home. Tired of her life of false respectability, Mrs. Heseltine determines at the end of the novel to enter the convent of the Blue Nuns in Rome and spend her life in repentance and attonement for her life of falsehood and deceit.

In Tynan's well-managed and fictional world, all must come full circle, all must be resolved. The guilty are punished, the weak excused, and those who hover between these two poles must make reparation. The remainder, those stock characters, round out their little lives with marriage and children, which, as from the beginning of her novel writing career, Tynan presents as the proper resolution of romantic plots.

X   Wives

Wives, published in 1924, is a collection of fourteen separate stories which have a number of secondary characters in common. As the title indicates, all of the stories deal with wives, women of different backgrounds, ages, characters, having in common the central experience of marriage. Most of the stories introduce issues which Tynan had seldom dealt with before. The opening tale, "Mrs. Jardine," describes the life of a woman living with her husband in a military settlement in India following the war. The women of the colony are bored, and in their boredom have taken to smoking, drinking, and flirting. Mrs. Jardine, always ready for a "rag," is foremost among them. Her language and openly seductive behavior is a new departure for a Tynan character. Her husband is disaffected because on the night their children died she had insisted on going to a dance and consequently was not at home when the children died. She, however, has suffered deeply, and it is only when two young girls come to visit her from Ireland that her true nature is restored and her marriage saved. "Mrs. Urquhart" tells of another young wife who lives in the Indian colony and who is tempted to leave her husband for another man. She is prevented from leaving by an accident of chance: her lover's car breaks down, and when her husband comes to the house she is relieved that she did not leave him. She knows that although he is a dull man, he truly loves her. In many of the stories the marriages of the wives are rescued from failure by unconvincing coincidence or weak psychological explanations. In two of the stories, however, the marriages actually founder, but Tynan, although willing to go as far as dealing with the subject of divorce, cannot condone what might follow after the divorce. In the story of "Mrs. Bennet," a young actress is happily married to Jim, an actor who falls in love with another woman. She divorces Jim so that he may marry the wwman who is to bear his child. The young actress then marries a Mr. Bennet in order to put a roof over her head and take care of her ailing mother. When her mother dies Mrs. Bennet realizes that she is unloved and unwanted by Mr. Bennet and his rich family. This situation had arisen because she had never believed in divorce or in remarriage and consequently she had not been able to believe in the validity of her marriage to Mr. Bennet. She grows gradually cold toward Mr. Bennet. On the night that she resolves to leave him secretly and forever, her first husband, Jim, unexpectedly arrives to see her. His wife and their child had died and he has realized that he never loved them as he had loved his first wife. They agree to go off together as man and wife because neither of them had believed in divorce and they still considered themselves to be very much married.

In "Mrs. Carstairs," Leila Carstairs is an extravagant, selfish woman whom Mr. Carstairs divorces with a great sense of relief. He has been in love with another woman, the gentle intelligent Audrey. Because he believes in the sacredness of marriage, however, he only allows himself to have a Platonic relationship with Audrey who loves him deeply. They remain soul companions and close friends for the rest of their lives, never marrying or living together.

These last two stories illustrate the ambivalence on Tynan's part when dealing with current social behavior. Although she attempts to confront such realistic issues as divorce, she does not deal in a realistic manner with either the causes or the consequences of these issues. Consequently, although some of her stories raise moral or ethical questions as serious as those of divorce or separation or remarriage, Tynan's management of her fictional world leaves these questions unresolved.

XI Sally Victrix

Throughout the period following the war in which Tynan wrote contemporary novels set in England or abroad, she also continued to deal with Irish characters and themes as well. Two of these Irish novels likewise deal with the changing status and roles of women.

In *Sally Victrix* (1921), Sally de Burgh is an Irish actress living in London with her father, Captain Burke, a very much decayed Irish gentleman. Through a theater critic, Mr. Follard, Sally meets Anthony Moylough, lord of Tramore, an Anglo-Irishman of noble line. He marries against his mother's wishes and takes Sally back to Ireland which she dreads because her father had disgraced the family name. He had tampered with racing horses in Ireland and had to leave in disgrace to live in England. Sally faces down society at her manorial home at Gurteen and rises in social estimation when Prince Paul, Anthony's godfather, pays her a visit. Her father is restored to her in Ireland after he reforms by performing brave deeds in Africa. The novel is meant to be a novel of manners and examines the operation of Anglo-Irish society and the feelings among the lower classes regarding religious differences. Sally is meant to appear as a girl of great moral fortitude, but the prose weakens her portrayal, with the book ending with the words: "So Sally faced the music for herself and those dearer to her than herself, and silenced it."

XII The House of Dreams

The last novel in this genre to be discussed is closely related in plot and characterization to *John Bulteel's Daughters* (1914) but the action is updated in *The House of Dreams* (1934) to accommodate Tynan's new audience. This novel, like *Sally Victrix*, looks at the lives of Irish girls living in England after the war. Like their English sisters, these girls have undergone the changes wrought in society. The story tells of Paddy Fitzgerald, an old blustery Irish widower living in England. His daughter Paula is the central character, and she is in love with Pierce Lacey, who dies of heart disease after a ten year courtship. She lives on with her dream of love in her house of dreams, Rose Cottage. Ursula, her elder sister, wants desperately to be a nun and refrains from her wish until her sisters are settled. Julia, the youngest, is a wild, stubborn girl given to doing whatever she wants. In the course of the novel both Julia and Paula go to Spain as governesses. This is a new departure for Tynan, reflecting the fact that women were beginning to travel alone and work for themselves. Julia falls in love with the captain of her boat on her return trip and marries him. Paula, after Pierce dies, rejects the love of Derek Warner who goes with his regiment to India where his wife and child die. Paula moves to South America, and when Derek gets out of the army, he pursues her there and they marry and raise a family.

In the course of the plot the mystery of the girls' antecedents is revealed. Their mother, the illegitimate daughter of a Lord Penreath and the woman who later became his wife, was raised by her mother's cousin, Lady Abervon, who knew the story and finally reveals it to the girls. This is one of the rare instances when Tynan dealt with the issue of illegitimacy, and it gives occasion for the characters to discuss at length both the initial shame they feel and their ultimate rejoicing in their heritage, and their long defense of love which accepts all things and overcomes all obstacles. Tynan's use of the device of the mysterious antecedents in this novel and in many others was closely related not only to the formula of romantic fiction but to her interest in the genre of the mystery or thriller.

XIII   *The Gothic Novels*

Early in Tynan's career she had shown a talent for the recounting of tales of suspense, such as the story of the death spancel in her early sketch of that title. In the last decade of her career Tynan turned again to the form of the gothic or thriller novel in a decision which anticipated the growing popularity of this form with the mass audience of the twentieth century. She wrote a small number of novels in this genre, making use of the traditional elements of gothic fiction: hints of the supernatural, isolation of the characters in the remote and wild countryside, large mysterious houses or castles, characters who border on the insane or the diabolical.

XIV   The Moated Grange

The Moated Grange (1926), reissued later as *The Night of Terror,* tells of Beata de Burgh and her mother, Delia. The fiction parallels the events of Tynan's own life in some measure, since it tells of the life of Delia, a young widow, whose husband's death in Ireland leaves her without a home or center to her existence. She travels with her daughter, and the description of their life together in London, moving from flat to flat, unhappy with the darkness, loneliness, and social isolation of urban life, mirrors Tynan's descriptions of her own life in London following her husband's death.

Delia's daughter, Beata, is writing a book, and the two women, hoping to escape from the drabness of London, undertake to rent the Moated Grange in Sussex, whose house and lake are apparently haunted. Most of the novel revolves around their terrifying experiences in this house whose caretaker, Mr. Crouch, is a drunkard, and whose cook, Mrs. Crouch, frightened her former employer to death. In the course of the action it further develops that Mr. Crouch had killed an old man whose decomposing body in the moat fills the house with evil odors. Since ordinary justice seldom plays a part in Tynan's novels, the plot has Crouch come to an evil end, battered to death by a windmill. Beata marries a young officer whose path had crossed hers in London and who finally rescues Beata and Delia from their unhappy situation. Wealthy and handsome, of course, he takes Beata away to reopen his family home in Ireland. Her mother, Delia, who is presented throughout as naive, cared for, and sheltered by her brave and intelligent daughter, marries the owner of the house, the wealthy and handsome Lord Egerton.

Tynan had a flair for suspense but, unfortunately, did not pursue it to any extent. She manages this plot fairly well, maintaining a real sense of horror throughout, but the exigencies of her formula demand that she provide the standard ending of a happy marriage for each of her two female characters, and the weak explanations of the motives of her evil doers.

One element of this novel, present in others written in this period, is the relationship of the older woman and the younger man, often the woman's son—the delicate love of the son, grown to manhood, for his mother. This devotion between mother and son, the loving and exclusive relationship which she perceived in Lord Edward's letters to his mother, and which is a major element of her fictional work, *Lord Edward: A Study in Romance* (1916), comes to replace, in many of her novels, the intense relationship between father and daughter. In addition to this change in the focus on certain relationships is Tynan's inclusion of strong relationships between mother and daughter, a theme which she had neglected in her early novels. Tynan's own relationship with her mother had been almost nonexistent;

however, as she aged, and as a mother herself, she developed a strong and loving relationship with her own daughter.

As Tynan began to run low on plots after many years of writing these romantic fictions, she lapsed into repeating plots of her earlier novels. One of these, perhaps unintentional, reworkings is *The Face in the Picture*, published in 1927, which repeats elements of the earlier *Denys the Dreamer* (1920). This novel also makes use of a central mystery and the workings of the supernatural at the same time as it incorporates into its action elements and features of the postwar life in England.

XV   The Face in the Picture

In *The Face in the Picture*, Dick Trevelyan, the young, handsome, and wealthy male leading character, stays at Crew with Austin Podmore and his father, a member of the nouveau riche, who has purchased the stately old mansion with some of his wartime profits as a men's outfitter. While visiting there, Dick sees an old portrait of a girl long dead, and later dreams she needs him and his help. Sometime after, he sees the same, and this time, living face on a shop model in a large London store. Following complicated clues, he discovers that the model, Dolly, is related to the artist who painted her face into the modern mural at the Podmore mansion. Pictured with her is a red-haired Judas-faced figure, Jasper Fleight, a master musician. Jasper is married to a scarred and disfigured Irish nurse living in England who, it develops, tended Dick when he was wounded in the war.

Meanwhile Dick's cousin, Lady Barbara, sees a wedding in a church through the medium of a crystal ball which is read to her. After more complications, Dick locates the house where Dolly had been living with another woman. After being hit over the head by an unknown assailant, he wakes up and remembers that the church described in the crystal ball is one which he had visited in France during the war. He rushes to France with Kate, Jasper's wife, arriving at the church in time to prevent the bigamous marriage between Dolly and Jasper who has her in thrall. Jasper, according to Tynan's natural justice, escapes the process of legal justice, but is killed in a car crash two days later. Dick marries Dolly who, it so happens, is a direct descendant of the great family of the Carews of Crew—thus the resemblance to the old portrait which initiated the plot.

This plot is formulaic, filled with coincidences, cliff hangers, visions, dreams. However, in Jasper, Tynan creates one of her very few genuinely evil characters whom she does not finally excuse. At the end of the book, a murdered woman, Jasper's victim, may still be in the millrace at Jasper's former hideout.

XVI The Rattlesnake

Another book in this vein is *The Rattlesnake*, whose plot, also, involves mysterious elements and complications. It is of interest because of the appearance of Dr. Melhuish, another master musician who has extraordinary powers over women. Characters such as Fleight and Melhuish, through the medium of their music, exert over these women a subjugating effect. The music is a transparent image for sexual attraction and sexual power. These books and the others like them, while retaining Tynan's standard plot and happy ending, incorporate into that plot elements of suspense, mild sexuality, modern occupations, and features such as cars and telephones in order to keep pace with the changing taste of her audience.

XVII Castle Perilous

Castle Perilous was published in 1928 and falls within the genre of the gothic suspense novel. It also raises issues regarding the role of women and has, as secondary themes, personal relationships which had occupied Tynan's work and thought in fiction for a number of years.

Castle Perilous, set on the Continent, includes scenes in the Tyrol (a favorite locale in the later novels), France, and Athens. It tells the story of Juliette Darell and her brother Jasper whose parents are dead and who are, consequently, independently wealthy, and heirs to a large estate in England called Longwood Beeches. At the opening of the story Juliette is visiting her English aunt in Beauport in France. Her brother Jasper is in the diplomatic corps in Athens as is her longtime friend and former lover, Denys Lester, who is married to an unworthy, flirtatious, and irresponsible but beautiful South American woman named Lola. In the course of her visit, Juliette encounters Maurice Greville who is in France in the care of an older woman. He is recovering from the shell shock he endured while fighting for England in World War I.

In the course of time, Juliette works out the complicated story of Maurice, a former student at the school of Denys attended. The woman who cares for him is a Dame Christine Dundas, known as Mrs. Smith, who had been the sister of the minister who ran the private school Maurice attended in his youth. As a child Maurice fell ill, and Miss Dundas took him to the Continent to recover. His mother found him and took him home. However, in the war Miss Dundas followed the troops to Europe and found Maurice in a field hospital. She took him away and cared for him, telling him in his weakened state that his own mother was dead. Out of illness and gratitude Maurice stays with her not knowing that she keeps him in a drugged state through her knowledge of herbs and potions. Whenever the world encroaches or she fears that he is slipping away from her, Miss Dundas takes Maurice to Castle Perilous in the Alps where she keeps him drugged and happy in one beautifully furnished room of the old castle. Christine Dundas (or Smith) does allow Maurice out for walks, and he becomes friendly with the monks who run a mountain hostel in their monastery in the Alps. The monks and the monastery ultimately feature in Maurice's rescue.

In the meanwhile Juliette meets Patrick O'Hara, an artist in Beauport who falls in love with her and with Nancy Carew, an Irish girl married to a former soldier who maltreats her owing to his war wounds and alcoholism. Juliette takes her little girl Bridget, thus enabling Nancy to travel as a companion to an American woman. Juliette takes Bridget and also Peter, Denys Lester's child, back to Longwood Beeches. She traces Christine's brother, the minister, in England and discovers that Maurice Greville's mother is still living. Together they travel by a circuitous route, following clues, to the Tyrol. Juliette stays in the monastery during a snow storm, and in the night is drawn by a mysterious sound to the dead room where the monks keep the bodies of those travelers who die on the mountain. She finds that the woman on the slab in the mortuary is not dead and comes to realize that the woman is Christine Smith for whom they have been searching. Before Miss Smith finally dies with a frozen baby in her arms, she tells Juliette that Maurice is drugged and hidden in the castle. Juliette is chased by wolves to the castle where she wanders about in the night and accidentally discovers a secret room where Maurice sleeps a sleep of death. She finds a secret drawer with a powder in it and a book which tells her how to revive Maurice, which she does by means of the powder.

Maurice is arrested for the death of Christine. Denys Lester arrives from South America where his wife has died. Patrick O'Hara arrives with Mrs. Greville who is reunited with her son. Maurice is cleared at his trial, and he takes his mother on a world cruise. Patrick O'Hara marries the newly widowed Nancy. Juliette marries Denys Lester and her brother Jasper marries another war widow and returns to Longwood Beeches. Christine's obsession with Maurice is shown to be a thwarted maternalism rather than the heretofore hinted at sexual passion of an older woman for a younger man.

Throughout the course of this long and complicated novel, many of the characters are spokesmen for ideas about women, especially Patrick O'Hara. In the following representative passage he is explaining to Juliette's aunt in Beauport his opinions on the women he has met since the war ended:

"Women are never cheap," he said. "There is so much in the world for a woman to do. You don't hear of unemployed women. Even those poor little girls who haunt such places as this in the season, dancing with old men and little boys and each other, some of them foolish and weary of life. God help them, there is work waiting to their hands if they will only find it and do it. There is no such thing as a superfluous woman."[3]

This brief summary of the plot of *Castle Perilous*, although leaving out many of the secondary characters and plot digressions, is sufficient to illustrate Tynan's attempts to incorporate into the novel not only gothic suspense, but her ideas on the status and role of women and contemporary thinking about society after the war. At the same time, she places the whole of the action and thought within her customary framework of the romantic novel which ends with the happy resolution of relationships and the marriage of the major and minor characters. Consequently, her work in the genre of the suspense novel cannot be considered as strictly gothic. The gothic elements, however, in these novels, make them of more interest to the modern reader than perhaps her more conventional formulaic romantic fictions. Because of the demands of the form, Tynan, of necessity, included major characters of an unusual nature — Christine Dundas (Smith) of course being one of these. In all of her novels of this gothic type she comes close to developing characters of real psychological interest, edging nearer to insight into character and motive than she customarily did in her romantic novels. Apparently, however, because of the nature of these characters, Tynan shies away from true or final analysis or the realistic portrayal of the characters in the culminating chapters and resorts instead to safe, socially acceptable and generous explanations for their actions or motives. Thus, in this genre of the suspense novel, as in her novels of romance and of realism, she presents the reader at the end with works of escapism. Although attempting in various ways to confront reality in these novels, reality of differing kinds according to the genre, she fails to follow through with her confrontation. Placing her audience's wish for entertainment and escapist fantasy beyond any other fictional, personal, or creative concern, Tynan manages her fiction so that it will always satisfy that one basic desire while merely touching upon the audience's other concerns.

The formula which she uncovered for herself and made her own in her early career sustained her through many decades of writing. Although in later life she turned, on occasion, to other fictional modes, the basic formula remained the same. Having succeeded, she continued to succeed. A clever, industrious, and prodigious writer she provided entertainment for herself and her audience, the pleasure of reading for them, and a means to support herself to the end of her long and active life.

XVIII *Conclusion*

Katharine Tynan, more than any reviewer or critic, clearly understood her own goals, her ability, and her limitations in the writing of her fiction. Practical and with few false ideas about her talent, and fully aware of the necessity of earning her own living, she saw her novels for what they were. In *Middle Years,* she is quite explicit about her intentions:

I have lived, to myself, by my poetry; or verse if you will. My innumerable novels were for boiling the pot. Not that I despise boiling the pot. The business might bear a worthier name. It might even be called a Holy War, the struggle to keep the fire on the hearth for the children, and the securities and sanctities of home about them. But my novels I wrote not to please myself, but to meet the demand; and the demand was diversified. Sometimes I wrote against the grain, as when I must purvey sensations to please readers of syndicated stories. My poetry, such as it is, I kept undefiled; and a good many people from time to time have liked to drink at its well.[4]

Tynan ably estimated her own intentions and ability in the writing of these novels. She had discovered a formula and wrote with speed and enjoyment. She created a large body of novels which gave pleasure, entertainment, and some instruction. She had no real literary ambitions in the genre as she had in her poetry. Given optimum conditions, it is unlikely that Tynan would have pursued novel writing to the extent that she did, pursuing it even to the detriment of her poetic talent. The enormous energy and vast amounts of time which these novels demanded may well have gone to produce more lasting work in poetry. That glorious adventure which Yeats saw her embark upon with her first prose work was to have consequences detrimental to her literary career in the end. Her "fatal facility," although reaping for her financial rewards when she needed them, was to do lasting damage to her literary commitment and, as a result, to her literary reputation. Today her novels can still be of interest when they are read in the context of her life and times; for in spite of all obstacles, she was one of the few women of her generation to support, successfully, herself and her life-style and all that that entailed, by the efforts of her pen.

CHAPTER 9

Summary

KATHARINE Tynan's literary career spanned over fifty years. During that half century, Ireland had emerged as an independent nation, and Europe had passed out of the nineteenth century into the postwar modern era. During those same years Tynan produced over one hundred and fifty published titles in the fields of poetry, fiction, and nonfiction. Her literary and personal fame reached its zenith early in her career and thereafter diminished with time and circumstance. Her literary reputation, however, has remained steady.

Tynan's contribution to the literature of her native Ireland in the late nineteenth century has been overshadowed in recent years by the dominant figure of W. B. Yeats. When seen in the context of those early years, however, her contribution, both personal and literary, was substantial. The great success of her first published work, *Louise de la Valliere*, served to encourage that coterie of new young writers in Ireland in the 1880s to continue, in their individual ways, to write and to publish. Tynan's ebullient personality, her enthusiasm, her personal generosity, and her willingness to encourage others and to share with them her experience, all contributed to the social life of that literary circle which had been centered at her beautiful home at Whitehall. That social and intellectual life, which centered for a time at Whitehall, helped to form the milieu in which W. B. Yeats' influential ideas took root and began to flourish.

Tynan's early works, particularly her first three volumes of poetry, place her in the forefront of the Irish literary revival. These volumes exhibit her intentions and her efforts to write a new kind of Irish poetry, poetry that was written in an Irish manner, on Irish themes, for an Irish audience. Her friendship with Yeats was important both in personal and literary terms. As the letters indicate, Yeats and Tynan, during a significant period of their early careers, shared with one another mutual support, encouragement, and intellectual stimulation. Tynan, with Yeats, saw the creative need to break with both English and European literary tradition and to establish an authentic and original Irish literature which would both reflect and contribute to the sense of Irish identity. Tynan's literary reputation as an Irish writer rests today primarily on those works which she produced during the peak of her early creativity and on her equal partnership with Yeats in establishing the Irish literary movement of the 1880s.

Tynan saw her own contribution to the world's literature to be her poetry, that genre which, as she says, she kept pure and undefiled. Following her early work in the Irish mode, Tynan turned from ethnic poetry to a more general style of poetry. She chose her subjects from the world of nature, or religious feeling, or the home and familial relationships. The best of these poems which she wrote on simple themes exhibit her fine eye for detail and observation; her excellent choice of images; her talent for compression and delicacy of statement; and her lyric sweetness. Apart from the Irish poems which establish her place in Irish literature, these simple poems establish Tynan, in world literature, as an important minor poet. Despite the passage of time, Tynan's "innocencies" still speak to the reader with a clear and simple voice. Within the body of her poetry, Tynan revealed her true personality with greater depth and sensitivity than in any other of her many fictional and nonfictional works. Of that poetry she herself wrote: "When I have been troubled about my own gift of poetry and have stood in the background, I have counted over those who have praised it: Bullen, Yeats, A. E., Francis Thompson, Alice Meynell, Louise Imogen Guiney, James Stephens—it is enough."[1]

The A. E. whom Tynan mentions in this passage was George Russell who wrote the introduction to his selection of Tynan's poetry (*Collected Poems,* 1930). As a personal friend, a mystic, and a poet himself, Russell had a particular insight into Tynan's life and poetry. His comments summarize her contributions to the world of poetry:

Katharine Tynan was the earliest singer in that awakening of our imagination which has been spoken of as the Irish Renaissance. I think she had as much natural sunlight in her as the movement ever attained.

. . . Katharine Tynan has her own spirituality, but she has kept closer to the normal than any except Padraic Colum. She had something which is rather rarer among poets than most people imagine, a natural gift for song. . . . I may be mistaken: but I think it has been easier for her to work in the craft of poetry than it has been with any of the poets I have known. But because it was easy and she has written many books of verse, it would do her wrong to think that what was written with a natural ease was not memorable. There was a mould in the psyche into which thought and emotion were poured, and the lyric record was almost always shapely. . . . She is happy in religion, friendship, children, flowers, in sky and clouds. She has, too, that spiritual bravery which makes beauty out of death or sorrow. . . . It is a great gift this, which on a sudden changes our gloom to glory, and only those have it who are born under a kind star.[2]

Katharine Tynan will be remembered for her contribution to poetry. Her novels do not stand as major works, nor did she intend them to be considered as such. However, they do stand as evidence of her enormous energy and resourcefulness, industry and imagination; for her commitment to providing a gracious and harmonious life for herself and her family and friends. Her success in the genre of romantic fiction and formulaic writing, and in all of her literary endeavors, is tribute to the talent, ambition, and ingenuity of that young girl from Clondalkin who burst upon the literary scene of Ireland and the world in 1885; the woman who created for herself a life of letters in what had been the bastion of male writers in the nineteenth century.

Her novels will fade into time, of interest only in terms of biography or literary history. Her many volumes of memoirs will survive as the living, readable record of a full life, and of the people and events which filled that life. The best of her poetry will live—filled as it is with delicate beauty, honesty, and the love of God and humanity.

Notes and References

Chapter One

1. Tynan, *Memories* (London, 1924), p. 386.
2. Ibid., p. 390.
3. Tynan, *Twenty-Five Years* (London, 1913), p. 27.
4. Ibid.
5. Ibid., p. 31.
6. Tynan, *Memories*, p. 396.
7. Ibid., p. 399.
8. Tynan, *Twenty-Five Years*, p. 23.
9. Letter received from Sister Prioress, Siena Convent, Drogheda, Ireland, November 25, 1977.
10. Tynan, *Twenty-Five Years*, p. 46.
11. Tynan, *Memories*, p. 399.
12. Ibid.
13. Tynan, *Twenty-Five Years*, p. 36.
14. Tynan, *The Middle Years* (London, 1916), p. 248.
15. Tynan, *Memories*, p. 402.
16. Tynan, *Twenty-Five Years*, p. 30.
17. Ibid.
18. Ibid., p. 24.
19. Tynan, *Memories*, p. 399.
20. Tynan, *Twenty-Five Years*, p. 41.
21. Ibid., p. 133.
22. Ibid., p. 41.
23. Ibid., p. 87.
24. Ibid., p. 70.
25. Ibid., p. 103.
26. Ibid., p. 283.
27. Ibid., p. 198.
28. Ibid., p. 145.
29. Douglas Hyde. This and subsequent diary entries quoted from Dominic Daly, *The Young Douglas Hyde: The Dawn of the Irish Revolution and Renaissance 1874–1893* (Dublin, 1974), p. 87.
30. Ibid., p. 88.
31. Ibid., p. 92.
32. Ibid., p. 93.
33. Ibid., p. 97.

34. W. B. Yeats, *The Bookman*, September, 1894.

35. Extract, Intermediate Education Board for Ireland, in *Book of Results* (Dublin), p. 202.

36. Letter received from Bernard Meehan, Manuscripts Assistant, Library of Trinity College Dublin, November 28, 1977.

37. Henry A. Hinkson, *A Student Life in Trinity College Dublin* (Dublin, 1892).

38. Henry A. Hinkson, ed., *Dublin Verses by Members of Trinity College* (Dublin, 1895). List of contributors includes Aubrey De Vere, Edward Dowden, Alfred Perceval Graves, Douglas Hyde, Standish O'Grady, Count Plunkett, T. W. Rolleston, John Todhunter, and Oscar Wilde.

39. "To Katharine Tynan," July 24, 1891, in *W. B. Yeats Letters to Katharine Tynan*, ed. Roger McHugh (Dublin, 1953), p. 129.

40. Tynan, *Twenty-Five Years*, p. 241.

41. Tynan, *The Middle Years*, p. 97.

42. Ibid., p. 98.

43. Letter received April 21, 1978, from the registrar of the National University of Ireland, established when the Royal University was dissolved by the 1908 Irish Universities Act.

44. Letter received from Commander R. S. Flynn, Sub-treasurer, The Honourable Society of the Inner Temple, quoting the records of the Inner Temple, London, England for 1902.

45. Tynan, *The Middle Years*, p. 99.

46. Tynan, *Twenty-Five Years; The Middle Years; The Years of the Shadow* (London, 1919); *The Wandering Years* (London, 1922); *Memories; Life in the Occupied Area* (London, 1925).

47. Tynan, *The Middle Years*, p. 294.

48. Ibid., p. 401.

49. Ibid., p. 205.

50. Ibid., p. 399.

51. Tynan, *The Years of the Shadow*, p. 269.

52. Tynan, *Memories*, p. 375.

53. Tynan, *The Wandering Years*, pp. 34–77.

54. Pamela Hinkson, ed., *Katharine Tynan: Selected Poems* (London, 1931), p. 30.

Chapter Two

1. Tynan, *Memories*, p. 25.

2. Tynan, *Twenty-Five Years*, p. 71.

3. Ibid., p. 103.

4. Treaty of Limerick (1691). The "Wild Geese" refers to Sarsfield and his men who left Ireland after the treaty.

5. *The Nation* was founded in 1842 by Sir Charles Gavan Duffy and was the organ of the Young Ireland party.

6. Tynan, *Louise de la Valliere* (London, 1885), p. 71.

7. "To Katharine Tynan," February 28, 1890, in *W. B. Yeats Letters to Katharine Tynan*, p. 111.

8. July, 1891, in ibid., p. 127.

9. Tynan, *A Nun, Her Friends and Her Order* (London, 1891), p. 45.

10. Ibid., p. 2.

11. Ibid., p. 94.

12. Tynan, *The Middle Years*, p. 100.

13. Ibid., p. 2.

14. Tynan, *Twenty-Five Years*, p. 71.

Chapter Three

1. Tynan, *Memories*, pp. 148–51.

2. Tynan, *Twenty-Five Years*, p. 143.

3. Ibid., p. 144.

4. Ibid., p. 145.

5. Ibid., p. 187.

6. Ibid., p. 189.

7. Tynan, *The Middle Years*, p. 12.

8. Tynan, *Twenty-Five Years*, p. 209.

9. Tynan, *Memories*, p. 260.

10. Henry Summerfield, *That Myriad Minded Man: A Biography of George W. Russell—A. E.* (Gerards Cross, England, 1975) p. 27. See also Tynan, *Twenty-Five Years*, p. 248.

11. *W. B. Yeats: Letters to Katharine Tynan*. Edited by Roger McHugh. (Dublin: Clonmore and Reynolds, 1953.)

12. Tynan, *The Middle Years*, p. 71.

13. Tynan, *Twenty-Five Years*, p. 150.

14. May 31, 1887, in *W. B. Yeats: Letters to Katharine Tynan*, p. 29.

15. Saturday, autumn, 1887, in ibid., p. 38.

16. May 19, 1888, in ibid., p. 56.

17. Saturday, August 13, 1887, in ibid., p. 38.

18. Wednesday, April 27, 1887, in ibid., p. 26.

19. Monday, February, 1888, in ibid., p. 46.

20. Ca. October 10, 1889, in ibid., p. 101.

21. Tuesday, December, 1889, in ibid., p. 106.

22. March 21, 1889, in ibid., p. 92.

23. July 24, 1891, in ibid., p. 129.

24. Ca. December 2, 1891, in ibid., p. 131.

25. Tynan, *Twenty-Five Years*, pp. 254–55.

26. May 1888, in *W. B. Yeats: Letters to Katharine Tynan*, p. 55.

27. December 21, 1888, in ibid., pp. 75–76.

28. March 21, 1889, in ibid., p. 92.

29. January 24, 1889, in ibid., p. 81.

30. August 1889, in ibid., pp. 99–100.

31. Ca. October 10, 1889, in ibid., p. 102.

32. Tynan, *The Middle Years*, p. 73.

33. W. B. Yeats, "Poems of Ellen O'Leary," in *Letters to the New Island,* ed. Horace Reynolds (Cambridge, Mass. 1934), p. 129.

34. March, 1895, in *W. B. Yeats: Letters to Katharine Tynan,* p. 143.

35. June 19, 1913, in ibid., p. 148.

36. Tynan, *Twenty-Five Years,* pp. 272–73.

Chapter Four

1. Tynan, *The Wild Harp: A Selection from Irish Lyrical Poetry* (London, 1913), p. 1.

2. George Brandon Saul, *Traditional Irish Literature* (Lewisburg, 1970), p. 51.

3. Tynan, *The Middle Years,* p. 316.

4. Ibid., p. 230.

5. Ibid., p. 352.

6. Tynan, *The Years of the Shadow,* p. 262.

7. George W. Russell, letter quoted in *The Middle Years,* p. 354.

Chapter Five

1. See *Some Experiences of an Irish R. M.* by E. Somerville and Martin Ross (pseud.), first published in 1899, for a humorous account of the Irish resident magistracy.

2. Tynan, *The Years of the Shadow,* p. 175.

3. Tynan, *Twenty-Five Years,* p. 1.

Chapter Six

1. Tynan, *The Middle Years,* p. 211.

2. W. B. Yeats, "Poetry and Patriotism," in *Poetry and Ireland: Essays by W. B. Yeats and Lionel Johnson.* (Dundrum, 1908), p. 3.

3. Tynan, Letter to James Joyce, May 24, 1914, in *The Cornell Joyce Collection Catalog,* comp. Robert E. Scholes (Ithaca, 1961), no. 585.

4. Tynan, *Peeps at Many Lands: Ireland* (London, 1914), p. 28.

5. Ibid., p. 26.

6. Ibid., p. 32.

7. Ibid., p. 36.

8. Ibid., p. 37.

9. Ibid., p. 19.

10. Tynan, *The Years of the Shadow,* p. 106.

11. Tynan, *Twenty-Five Years,* p. 14.

12. Tynan, *The Middle Years,* p. 226.

13. Tynan, *Twenty-Five Years,* p. 122.

14. Tynan, *The Wandering Years,* p. 120.

15. Tynan, *The Middle Years,* p. 383.

16. Tynan, *The Wandering Years,* p. 127.

17. Tynan, *Memories*, p. 361.
18. Ibid., p. 380.
19. Tynan, *Twenty-Five Years*, p. 16.
20. Tynan, *The Middle Years*, p. 268.
21. Tynan, *Memories*, p. 5.

Chapter Seven

1. Tynan, *Memories*, p. 295.
2. Tynan, *The Middle Years*, p. 7.
3. Tynan, *A Cluster of Nuts* (London, 1894), p. 11.
4. Ibid., p. 99.
5. Thomas Flanagan, *The Irish Novelists 1800-1850* (New York, 1959).
6. Tynan, *The Middle Years*, p. 110.
7. Ibid., p. 121.
8. Tynan, *The Way of a Maid* (London, 1895), p. 6.
9. Tynan, *The Wandering Years*, p. 228.
10. Elaine Showalter, *A Literature of Their Own* (Princeton, 1977), p. 7.
11. Ibid., p. 20.
12. Tynan, *The Way of a Maid*, p. 6.
13. Tynan, *The Middle Years*, p. 96.
14. Tynan, *The Dear Irish Girl* (London, 1899), p. 70.
15. Northrop Frye, *The Secular Scripture: A Study of the Structure of Romance* (Cambridge, Mass., 1976), p. 68.
16. Showalter, *A Literature of Their Own*, p. 158.
17. John G. Cawelti, *Adventure, Mystery, and Romance: Formula Stories as Art and Popular Culture* (Chicago, 1976), pp. 35-36.
18. Cawelti, *Adventure, Mystery, and Romance*, pp. 41-42.
19. August 13, 1887, in *W. B. Yeats: Letters to Katharine Tynan*, p. 38.
20. Tynan, *Cabinet of Irish Literature* (London, 1902), p. 24.

Chapter Eight

1. Tynan, *Life in the Occupied Area*, p. 139.
2. Tynan, *The Respectable Lady* (London, 1927), p. 303.
3. Tynan, *Castle Perilous* (London, 1928), p. 41.
4. Tynan, *The Middle Years*, p. 353.

Chapter Nine

1. Tynan, *The Wandering Years*, p. 268.
2. George Russell, ed., *Collected Poems by Katharine Tynan* (London, 1930), pp. vii-xiii.

Selected Bibliography

1. Novels and Stories

The Adventures of Alicia. London: F. V. White and Co., 1906.

The Briar Bush Maid. London: Ward, Lock and Co., 1926.

Castle Perilous. London: Ward, Lock and Co., 1928.

A Cluster of Nuts: Being Sketches Among My Own People. London: Lawrence and Bullen, 1894.

Connor's Wood. London: Collins, 1933. Revised and completed by P. Hinkson.

Countrymen All: A Collection of Tales. London: Maunsel and Co., Ltd., 1915.

Cousins and Others:Tales. London: T. Werner Laurie, 1909.

A Daughter of the Fields. London: Smith, Elder and Co., 1900.

The Dear Irish Girl. London: Smith, Elder and Co., 1899.

Delia's Orchard. London: Ward, Lock and Co., 1931.

Denys the Dreamer. London: Ward, Lock and Co., 1920.

Dick Pentreath. London: Smith, Elder and Co., 1905.

The Face in the Picture. London: Ward, Lock and Co., 1927.

A Fine Gentleman. London: Ward, Lock and Co., 1929.

The Forbidden Way. London: W. Collins Sons and Co., 1931.

The French Wife. London: F. V. White and Co., 1904.

A Girl of Galway. London: Blackie, 1902.

The Golden Lily. New York: Benziger Bros. and Son, 1899.

The Golden Rose. London: Nash and Grayson, 1924.

*Grayson's Girl.*London: W. Collins Sons and Co., 1930.

The Handsome Quaker and Other Stories. London: A. H. Bullen, 1902.

Haroun of London. London: Collins, 1927.

The Heiress of Wyke. London: Ward, Lock and Co., 1926.

Her Ladyship. London: Smith, Elder and Co., 1907.

Her Mother's Daughter. London: Smith, Elder and Co., 1909.

Honey, My Honey. London: Smith, Elder and Co., 1912.

The Honourable Molly. 1903; reprint London: John Murray, 1914.

The House in the Forest. London: Ward, Lock and Co., 1928.

The House of the Crickets. London: Smith, Elder and Co., 1908.

The House of Dreams. London: Ward, Lock and Co., 1934.

The House of the Foxes. London: Smith, Elder and Co., 1915.

The Infatuation of Peter. London: W. Collins, 1926.

An International Marriage. London: Ward, Lock and Co., 1933.

An Isle in the Water: Short Stories. London: A. and C. Black, 1895.

John-A-Dreams. London: Smith, Elder and Co., 1916.
John Bulteel's Daughters. London: Smith, Elder and Co., 1914.
Julia. London: Smith, Elder and Co., 1904.
A King's Woman. London: Hurst and Blackett, 1902.
Kit. London: Smith, Elder and Co., 1917.
A Lad was Born. London: Collins, 1934.
The Land of Mist and Mountain: Short Stories. London: Unwin Bros., 1895.
A Little Radiant Girl. London: Blackie and Son, 1914.
A Lonely Maid. London: Ward, Lock and Co., 1931.
Lord Edward Fitzgerald: A Study In Romance. London: Smith, Elder and Co., 1916.
Love of Brothers. London: Constable and Co., 1919.
Love of Sisters. London: Smith, Elder and Co., 1902.
Lover of Women. London: W. Collins Sons and Co., 1928.
The Luck of the Fairfaxes. London: Collins, Clear Type Press, 1905.
The Man From Australia. London: W. Collins and Co., 1919.
Margery Dawe. London: Blackie and Sons, 1916.
Mary Beaudesert, V.S. London: W. Collins Sons and Co., 1923.
A Midsummer Rose. London: Smith, Elder and Co., 1913.
Miss Gascoigne. London: John Murray, 1917.
Miss Mary. London: John Murray, 1917.
Miss Phipps. London: Ward, Lock and Co., 1925.
The Moated Grange. London: W. Collins Sons and Co., 1926.
The Most Charming Family. London: Ward, Lock and Co., 1929.
My Love's But a Lassie. London: Ward, Lock and Co., 1918.
The Night of Terror. Originally published as *The Moated Grange.*
Oh, What a Plague is Love. London: Black, 1896.
The Other Man. London: Ward, Lock and Co., 1932.
Pat the Adventurer. London: Ward, Lock and Co., 1923.
Peggy, the Daughter. London: Cassell and Co., 1909.
The Pitiful Lady. London: Ward, Lock and Co., 1932.
The Playground. London: Ward, Lock and Co., 1932.
Princess Katharine. London: Ward, Lock and Co., 1912.
The Rattlesnake. London: Ward, Lock and Co., 1917.
A Red, Red Rose. London: Eveleigh Nash, 1903.
The Respectable Lady. London: Collins, 1927.
The Rich Man. London: W. Collins Sons and Co., 1929.
The River. London: W. Collins Sons and Co., 1929.
The Rose of the Garden. Indianapolis: Bobbs-Merrill, 1913.
Sally Victrix. London: W. Collins Sons and Co., 1921.
The Second Wife and *A July Rose.* London: John Murray, 1921.
She Walks in Beauty. London: Smith, Elder and Co., 1899.
Since First I Saw Your Face. London: Hutchinson and Co., 1915.
The Story of Cecilia. London: Smith, Elder and Co.. 1911.

The Story of Our Lord for Children. Dublin: Sealy, Bryers and Co., 1907.
That Sweet Enemy. Philadelphia: Lippincott, 1901.
They Loved Greatly. London: E. Nash and Grayson, 1923.
A Union of Hearts. London: J. Nisbet and Co., 1901.
The Way of a Maid. London: Lawrence and Bullen, 1895.
The Web of Fraulein. London: Hodder and Stoughton, 1916.
White Ladies. London: E. Nash and Grayson, 1922.
The Wild Adventure. London: Ward, Lock and Co., 1927.
Wives. London: Hurst-Blackett, 1924.
The Yellow Domino and Other Stories. London: F. V. White, 1906.

2. Poetry
Ballads and Lyrics. London: Kegan Paul and Co., 1891.
Cuckoo Songs. London: E. Mathews and J. Lane, 1894.
Evensong. Oxford: Basil Blackwell, 1922.
Experiences. London: A. H. Bullen, 1908.
The Flower of Peace: A Collection of Devotional Poetry. London: Burns and Oates, 1914.
Flower of Youth: Poems in War Time. London: Sidgwick and Jackson, Ltd., 1915.
Herb O'Grace: Poems in Wartime. London: Sidgwick and Jackson, Ltd., 1918.
The Holy War. London: Sidgwick and Jackson, Ltd., 1916.
Innocencies: A Book of Verse. London: A. H. Bullen, 1905.
Irish Poems. London: Sidgwick and Jackson, Ltd., 1913.
Late Songs. London: Sidgwick and Jackson, Ltd., 1917.
Lauds. London: The Cedar Press, 1909.
A Little Book of XXIV Carols. Portland, Maine: Thomas Mosher, 1907.
Louise de la Valliere. London: Kegan Paul, Trench and Co., 1885.
A Lover's Breast-Knot. London: Elkin Mathews, 1896.
New Poems. London: Sidgwick and Jackson, 1911.
Poems. London: Lawrence and Bullen, Ltd., 1901.
Poems and Ballads of Young Ireland. London: M. H. Gill and Son, 1890.
The Rhymed Life of St. Patrick. London: Burns and Oates, 1907.
Shamrocks. London: Kegan Paul, Trench and Co., 1887.
Twilight Songs. Oxford: Blackwell, 1927.
The Wind in the Trees: A Book of Country Verse. London: Grant Richards, 1898.

3. Collected Poetry.
Collected Poems. Foreword by George Russell. London: Macmillan and Co., Ltd., 1930.
The Poems of Katherine [sic] Tynan. Edited with an introduction by Monk Gibbon. Dublin: Allen Figgis, 1963.

Selected Poems. Introduction by P. Hinkson. Augustan Books of Poetry. London: Ernest Benn, 1931.

4. Nonfiction and Collections Edited by Tynan
A Book of Irish History. Dublin: Educational Company of Ireland, 1918.
A Book of Memory. London: Hodder and Stoughton, 1906.
A Cabinet of Irish Literature. 2d ed. London: Gresham Publishing Company, 1902.
Father Matthew. London: MacDonald and Evans, 1910.
Ireland: Peeps at Many Lands. London: A. and C. Black, 1914.
Irish Love Songs: Selected by K. Tynan. London: T. Fisher Unwin, 1892.
A Little Book for John O'Mahony's Friends. Portland, Maine: Thomas Mosher, 1909.
A Little Book for Mary Gill's Friends. Petersfield, England: Pear Tree Press, 1906.
A Nun, Her Friends and Her Order. London: Kegan Paul and Co., 1891.
The Wild Harp: A Selection from Irish Poetry. London: Sidgwick and Jackson, 1913.

5. Other Collections
Maxims from the Writings of Katharine Tynan. Selected by Elsie E. Morton. The Angelus Series. London: R. and T. Washbourne, 1916.

6. Autobiographical Works
Life in the Occupied Area. London: Hutchinson and Co., 1925.
Memories. London: Eveleigh Nash, 1924.
The Middle Years. London: Constable and Co., 1916.
Twenty-Five Years: Reminiscences. London: Smith, Elder and Co., 1913.
The Wandering Years. London: Constable and Co., Ltd.; New York: Houghton Mifflin Co., 1922.
The Years of the Shadow. London: Constable and Co., Ltd., 1919.

7. Books by Henry A. Hinkson
The Considine Luck. London: Stephen Swift and Co., Ltd., 1912.
Copyright Law. London: A. H. Bullen, 1903.
Dublin Verses by Members of Trinity College. Edited by H. A. Hinkson. Dublin: Hodges, Figgis and Co., Ltd., 1895.
Golden Lads and Girls. London: Downey and Co., Ltd., 1895.
Golden Morn. London: Cassell and Co., Ltd., 1907.
A Student Life in Trinity College Dublin. Dublin: J. Charles and Son, 1892.

8. Correspondence by W. B. Yeats
Letters to the New Island. Edited by Horace Reynolds. Cambridge: Harvard University Press, 1934.

W. B. Yeats: Letters to Katharine Tynan. Edited by Roger McHugh. Dublin: Clonmore and Reynolds, 1953.

SECONDARY SOURCES

Anon. *A Round Table of the Representative Irish and English Catholic Novelists*. New York: Benziger Bros., 1897. A collection of short stories and excerpts from novels including a story by Katharine Tynan and a picture and biographical sketch.

BOYD, ERNEST A. *Ireland's Literary Renaissance*. New York: John Lane Co., 1916. Contemporary study of the movement which has become a standard work; includes critical comments on Tynan's writings and her place in the movement.

BROWN, STEPHEN J. *Ireland in Fiction: A Guide to Irish Novels, Tales, Romances and Folklore*. 1915; reprint Ireland: Dublin University Press, 1969. Includes summaries of a number of Tynan's novels set in Ireland.

CARVER, GEORGE. ed, *The Catholic Tradition in English Literature*. New York: Doubleday, Page and Co., 1926. This collection of representative passages of poetry by Catholic poets writing in English gives an indication of the tradition of Catholic poetry in which Katharine Tynan wrote.

CASEY, DANIEL, and RHODES, ROBERT, eds. *Views of the Irish Peasantry 1800-1916*. Hampden, Conn: Archon Books, 1977. A collection of essays dealing with the Irish peasant.

CAWELTI, JOHN C. *Adventure, Mystery, and Romance: Formula Stories as Art and Popular Culture*. Chicago: University of Chicago Press, 1976. The first two chapters in particular are useful to the student.

DALY, DOMINIC. *The Young Douglas Hyde: The Dawn of the Irish Revolution and Renaissance 1874-1893*. Dublin: Irish University Press, 1974. Biographical study of the early and formative years of Douglas Hyde containing excerpts from Hyde's diaries and letters.

FLANAGAN, THOMAS. *The Irish Novelists: 1800-1850*. New York: Columbia University Press, 1959. Excellent study of the course of the Irish novel. Provides historical background and studies Edgworth, Banim, Griffin, Carleton, and Lady Morgan.

GWYNN, STEPHEN. *Irish Literature and Drama in the English Language: A Short History*. New York: Nelson and Son, 1936. Well-known history of the movement written close enough to the period to retain the freshness of contemporary opinion.

MARCUS, PHILIP L. *Yeats and the Beginning of the Irish Renaissance*. Ithaca: Cornell University Press, 1970. Places Yeats in relation to his youthful contemporaries, Tynan among them.

MOERS, ELLEN. *Literary Women: The Great Writers*. New York:

Anchor Press/Doubleday, 1977. Feminist study of English, American and continental female writers of the nineteenth and twentieth centuries.

PERKINS, DAVID. *A History of Modern Poetry.* Cambridge: Harvard University Press, 1978. Places the Irish Literary Renaissance in the wider context of twentieth-century poetry.

SHOWALTER, ELAINE. *A Literature of Their Own: British Women Novelists from Bronte to Lessing.* Princeton: Princeton University Press, 1977. Excellent scholarly study of the female tradition in English literature. Provides historical and sociological information as well as literary criticism.

SUMMERFIELD, HENRY. *That Myriad Minded Man: A Biography of G. W. Russell—A. E.* Gerards Cross, England: Colin Symthe, 1975. Thorough introduction to the life and work of a complex Irishman.

Index